# Tales of Power

## Michael Berman

www.learbooks.co.uk

This first edition published by:
Lear Books
Windrush House
High Tor West
Earl Shilton
Leics
LE9 7DN
UK



Cover design by Paul Mason

ISBN 978-1-907614-05-7

Printed in England by Booksprint.

## Contents

## Introduction
## THE ART OF STORYTELLING

Jürgen Kremer, transpersonal psychologist and spiritual practitioner, defines tales of power as conscious verbal constructions based on numinous experiences in non-ordinary reality, "which guide individuals and help them to integrate the spiritual, mythical, or archetypal aspects of their internal and external experience in unique, meaningful, and fulfilling ways" (Kremer, 1988, p.192). Such stories can broaden our horizons, connect us to a vision and provide an overarching narrative for our journeys through life, and it is stories of this type that form the focus of this book.

The stories painted or drawn on the walls of caves in petroglyphs and told around the prehistoric campfires were man's first form of education, communication, entertainment and healing, far pre-dating the written word. The Twelve Tribes of Israel used the oral tradition for centuries in passing down the parables of the Creation and Noah's Flood, and it was not until King Solomon decreed that these stories be written down that we had any records from which much of the "Old Testament" was taken. It can be argued that we have a responsibility to carry on this tradition and that mankind has a need for storytellers that is almost as great as his need for love.

Like the shaman, the storyteller is a walker between the worlds, a mediator between our known world and that of the unknown - someone who is able to commune with dragons and elves, with faeries and angels, with magical and mythical beasts, with Gods and Goddesses, heroes and demons; someone who is able to pass freely from this world into those above and those below and to help us to experience those other realms for ourselves. He or she is an intensely powerful invoker of elemental powers, of the powers of absolute transformation, who can show us how to confront our most deeply-engrained fears, teach us how to experience ecstasy, bring us face to face with death or terror of the spirit - with the infinite and incomprehensible. He is not only the archetypal magician but also the archetypal guide.

In many traditions, storytelling is synonymous with song, chant, music or epic poetry, especially in the bardic traditions. Stories may be chanted or sung, along with musical accompaniment on a certain instrument. Therefore those called folk musicians by foreign music enthusiasts could just as well be called storytellers - their true roles being more profound, as their names reflect: bards, *ashiks, jyrau, griots* amongst many more. Their roles, in fact, are often as much spiritual teachers or healers - for which the stories and music are vehicles - as well as historians and tradition-bearers.

In Central Asia, for example, the same Turkic term, *bakhshi*, may be used for both shamans and bards, and both may be called to their trade by spirits after a difficult period of initiation. Indeed a bard can be described as a healer who uses music as a gateway to the world of the Spirit, and there is a magical dimension to reciting the epics. They use a fiddle or lute as accompaniment, and tales may run through several nights of exhaustive performance. For genuine initiates of these bardic disciplines, they draw directly on the conscious creative power of the Divine and transmit it through the words they speak and sing. This is not the same as merely being creative or feeling inspired and involves considerable spiritual training.

In Turkey, the folk-poets of Anatolia are usually referred to as ashiks, meaning 'the ones in love' (with the Divine). The ashiks, who belong to the Bektasi / Alevi faith, have wandered the plains of Anatolia since around the tenth century. They accompany themselves on the *saz*, a long-necked lute with three sets of strings, said to represent the fundamental trinity of the Muslim faith: Allah, Mohammed and Ali.

However, there is no need to travel so far afield in search of the storyteller as shaman. Ballads such as *Thomas Rhymer*, as close analysis shows, are in fact shamanic journeys in themselves It is the kiss from the Queen of fair Elfland that moves what Carlos Castaneda called the 'assemblage point' and initiates the process of the journey. As Castaneda explains through the teachings of Don Juan, what we call 'reason' is merely a by-product of the habitual position of the assemblage point. Dreaming (and / or visualization) gives us the fluidity to enter into other worlds and to perceive the inconceivable by making the assemblage point shift outside the human domain. The Child ballad (variant 37C) is presented below, followed by more detailed analysis:

**37C: Thomas Rymer**

37C.1 TRUE Thomas lay on Huntlie bank,
A ferlie he spied wi' his ee,
And there he saw a lady bright,

Come riding down by the Eildon Tree.
37C.2 Her shirt was o the grass-green silk,
Her mantle o the velvet fyne,
At ilka tett of her horse's mane
Hang fifty siller bells and nine.
37C.3 True Thomas, he pulld aff his cap,
And louted low down to his knee:
'All hail, thou mighty Queen of Heaven!
For thy peer on earth I never did see.'
37C.4 'O no, O no, Thomas,' she said,
'That name does not belang to me;
I am but the queen of fair Elfland,
That am hither come to visit thee.
37C.5 'Harp and carp, Thomas,' she said,
'Harp and carp along wi me,
And if ye dare to kiss my lips,
Sure of your bodie I will be.'
37C.6 'Betide me weal, betide me woe,
That weird shall never daunton me;'
Syne he has kissed her rosy lips,
All underneath the Eildon Tree.
37C.7 'Now, ye maun go wi me,' she said,
'True Thomas, ye maun go wi me,
And ye maun serve me seven years,
Thro weal or woe, as may chance to be.'
37C.8 She mounted on her milk-white steed,
She's taen True Thomas up behind,
And aye wheneer her bridle rung,
The steed flew swifter than the wind.
37C.9 O they rade on, and farther on-+-
The steed gaed swifter than the wind-+-
Untill they reached a desart wide,
And living land was left behind.
37C.10 'Light down, light down, now, True Thomas,
And lean your head upon my knee;
Abide and rest a little space,
And I will shew you ferlies three.
37C.11 'O see ye not yon narrow road,

So thick beset with thorns and briers?
That is the path of righteousness,
Tho after it but few enquires.
37C.12 'And see not ye that braid braid road,
That lies across that lily leven?
That is the path of wickedness,
Tho some call it the road to heaven.
37C.13 'And see not ye that bonny road,
That winds about the fernie brae?
That is the road to fair Elfland,
Where thou and I this night maun gae.
37C.14 'But, Thomas, ye maun hold your tongue,
Whatever ye may hear or see,
For, if you speak word in Elflyn land,
Ye'll neer get back to your ain countrie.'
37C.15 O they rade on, and farther on,
And they waded thro rivers aboon the knee,
And they saw neither sun nor moon,
But they heard the roaring of the sea.
37C.16 It was mirk mirk night, and there was nae stern light,
And they waded thro red blude to the knee;
For a' the blude that's shed on earth
Rins thro the springs o that countrie.
37C.17 Syne they came on to a garden green,
And she pu'd an apple frae a tree:
'Take this for thy wages, True Thomas,
It will give the tongue that can never lie.'
37C.18 'My tongue is mine ain,' True Thomas said;
'A gudely gift ye wad gie to me!
I neither dought to buy nor sell,
At fair or tryst where I may be.
37C.19 'I dought neither speak to prince or peer,
Nor ask of grace from fair ladye:'
'Now hold thy peace,' the lady said,
'For as I say, so must it be.'
37C.20 He has gotten a coat of the even cloth,
And a pair of shoes of velvet green,
And till seven years were gane and past
True Thomas on earth was never seen.

It is the kiss of the Queen of fair Elfland that changes the life of Thomas Rhymer forever, as the start of his descent into what can be regarded as the Lower World of the shaman is marked by that kiss. The Fairy Queen tells Thomas of the three paths that lie ahead and explains the meaning to him, acting as a guide or sacred teacher.

The first path is almost desert, flat, wide and straight as far as the eye can see. Although easy to journey on, it is of absolutely no consequence. It would appear to be a reference to an occupation that is easy and so leads to no rewards, expanding neither knowledge nor skill and devoid of any spiritual value. It offers a contrast to the traditional path of an initiate into shamanic practices, who often has to undergo great suffering and hardship along the way.

The second path is narrow, winding and treacherous with thorny hedges encroaching on both sides. Hazardous in the extreme, yet with a happy ending for it leads to the city of the kings. As we know, the king is always at the centre and in control. The suggestion is that after all the trials and tribulations of endangering oneself and surviving on a path upon which many obstacles are encountered, the reward for the righteous is entrance to the king, an honour indeed.

The third path is lush and green, meandering into forest and glade. It is a wild place where one could easily get lost. The Queen gives no explanation of this and quite simply says "This is the path to Fairy Land, and do not utter a world whilst in this land or you will end up staying forever." This suggests that anything spoken in the otherworld is to be taken very seriously indeed.

**The Soul Journey and the Storyteller**

The only material thing Thomas is given on his journey is an enchanted harp and it is used as a link between the two worlds. It can be regarded as the equivalent of the shaman's drum, the rhythmic beating of which is used to induce a trance state. In some cultures a musical bow was plucked in a rhythmic way to achieve the same state, and in others songs were sung. The Sufis use dance to produce the same effects. Other parallels can also be drawn between the ballad of *Thomas Rhymer* and a shamanic journey but limitation of space precludes further analysis here (see Berman, 2011, for this).

Significantly, a link has been established by Peggy Ann Wright at Lesley College in Cambridge, Massachusetts, between heightened temporal lobe activity and shamanistic experiences. These are soul journeys to distant realms of experience in order to communicate with spirits, and to bring back healing advice. Rhythmic drumming of the sort used in a vast range of spiritual rituals excites the temporal lobes and associated areas of the limbic system, as can the practice of guided visualization. Moreover, each time a storyteller introduces a tale starting ‘once upon a time’, he / she is inviting the audience to transcend their linear concepts of time and space, and so enter a light state of trance. Consequently, as in the case of shamanic journeying and guided visualisation, storytelling can also be used to facilitate the development of what Zohar (2000) calls Spiritual Intelligence - what we use to develop our longing and capacity for meaning, vision and value.

**Becoming a Storyteller**

As a storyteller, it is obviously important to know your story but this does not necessarily mean memorizing the words. You can do that if you want to, but the main thing is to know what happens to whom and when it is supposed to happen. One way of accomplishing this is to make an outline of the story to study. Another way is to imagine a picture for each part of the story with all the important things in the picture. Any special parts of the presentation such as poetry or complex phrases can be learned by heart and / or you can print them out on cue cards for reference. The more you repeat them out loud, the easier it will be to say them, whether you memorize them or not. Use stories you are confident with from previous occasions for a first time situation because the knowledge that you are well prepared helps diminish any nervousness you might be experiencing.

Before it is time to tell, if possible, check out the space. If there is something that needs to be set up or changed, something to be planned, do it early, before you tell. Anticipate some of the things which might go wrong and know the strategies you will use to deal with any problems that might crop up. Make sure you have a fall-back position or some extra material up your sleeve to use if necessary. Remember that most of the things which are not right will probably only be noticed by you. Deal with everything you need to deal with beforehand, but then forget about those things. When you get up to tell, it is time to concentrate on the listeners.

Keep the introduction and explanation as brief as possible. You may want to memorize some opening lines to make sure you leave nothing to chance and to show the audience that you know what you are doing; from then on it is up to them. As for the ending, take your time, but not the next speaker’s. Be on, be good, and be off (vaudevillians’ rule). Prepare a clean punch line or closing comment to finish with. “And that’s the story of __,” will do. And remember to thank your audience too.

Making mistakes is a natural part of performing. It is not a question of what to do if you make a mistake, but simply a matter of when you make a mistake. The most important thing is to stay calm and keep going. The audience does not know you have made a mistake unless you tell them, so do not draw attention to the problem by admitting to it or apologising. As far as they know, the way you told the story is the way you meant to tell it.

When you look out at the people listening to you, avoid anyone who makes you nervous. Try to find the people who make you feel safe. There is no reason to be scared of your audience. Your audience is (usually) your friend. They want you to succeed. And, since many of them are also nervous about talking in front of people, they will be sympathetic if things go wrong. Obviously, this sympathy is somewhat dependent on the venue and how much people pay to see you perform.

The nervousness you feel before going on is your performance energy. That is what will get you up on stage and into your story. And if you do not feel it, your performance will probably fall flat. The energy you feel is an instinctive reaction to stress. The body knows that something is about to happen and is preparing for action. However, the emotional content is entirely conscious. Research shows that physiologically, fear, anger and excitement are all identical; the body is reacting in the same way. Your mind determines how you react to those stimuli and your emotions are under your control. With some practice, you can control whether it is fear or excitement running through your head before going on.

If you suffer badly from nerves, the Zen concept of No-Self as an approach to the problem can prove to be helpful - "There is no teller... only the tale." In this way you disappear for yourself as well as for the listeners. And if you have disappeared then there is no one to be nervous for.

An alternative approach is to make use of a Talking Stick (an American Indian tradition) which you pick up when you tell and hand to others when they tell. It helps to connect you to those legions over the centuries who have told stories and to remind you that you have an ancient responsibility to both audience and story. This carries you well beyond the awareness of nervousness. The nervousness is still there but now it is harnessed to bringing out the life in that story. The idea is to make your focus the responsibility to your audience and your story, rather than focusing on yourself. Let go of yourself and think about the people you are telling the story to. Pay attention to them and you won't be thinking of yourself and you won't be nervous.

Guided visualisation can also be an effective tool. Sitting in some quiet place, imagine as clearly as possible that you are preparing to perform, employing all your senses - the sights, sounds, smells and feelings associated with these pre-performance moments. Be as specific and detailed in your imaging as possible. When you have placed yourself as fully as possible into the pre-performance context, imagine yourself feeling completely confident-fearless. Imagine how great it would be to feel that way, rather than scared. Then continue on with the imagined performance: you present your material - solidly, and with confidence. Imagine the smoothness and grace with which you will make your presentation. Imagine your heart keeping a steady pace instead of racing. Imagine your breath deep and full, not shallow and shaky. In other words, paint an accurate and detailed mental image of every step of the process - the way you've experienced it so many times before - but with a successful outcome. Once you have experienced success in non-ordinary reality in this way, it becomes that much easier to achieve in this reality.

Slowing down your breathing can help to control nervousness too. If you must focus on yourself, then focus on your breath. Breathing is the most important thing for life. If you are nervous, if you are scared or feel anyway you don't want to feel, then think about your breath and control it. Deep breaths, in through your nose and out through your mouth. Once you have your breath under control, you can do anything.

One way to practise storytelling with others is to pick a partner and sit facing each other, close enough to have your knees touching. Have other partners on either side of you so you are in two long lines all up close against each other, and all facing your respective partners. One person in each pair starts the story and after thirty seconds to a minute say 'and', and then 'throw' the story to the person opposite to continue. That person makes up the next short segment, says 'and' and then passes the story back to the first person again. The story unfolds by being passed backwards and forwards this way between the same two partners.

Before everyone starts they are told that the story that is to unfold between each pair is to be about a journey. Two people who are very fond of each other go their separate ways and on their respective journeys. Many things happen during the course of their journeys that stretch their resourcefulness and help them grow in wisdom. Then circumstances happen such that they find each other again and share the experiences they had along the way.

**Bibliography**

Berman, M. (2011) *Shamanic Journeys, Shamanic Stories*, Hampshire: O Books.

Child, F. J. (1886-98) *The English and Scottish Popular Ballads*, Boston, New York, Houghton, Mifflin and Company. Ballads originally transcribed by Cathy Lynn Preston. HTML Formatting at sacred-texts.com. This text is in the public domain. These files may be used for any non-commercial purpose, provided this notice of attribution is left intact.

Kremer, J.W. (1988) "Shamanic Tales as Ways of Personal Empowerment." In Doore, G. (ed.) *Shaman's Path: Healing, Personal Growth and Empowerment*, Boston, Massachusetts: Shambhala Publications.

Sheppard, T., http://www.timsheppard.co.uk/story/ Tim Sheppard's Storytelling Resources for Storytellers.

Zohar, H., & Marshall, I., (2000) *Spiritual Intelligence The Ultimate Intelligence*, Bloomsbury, London.

## Chapter 1
## THE ORIGIN OF STORIES
(Told by Henry Jacob) [1]

This happened long ago, in the time of our forefathers.

In a Seneca village lived a boy whose father and mother died when he was only a few weeks old. The little boy was cared for by a woman, who had known his parents. She gave him the name of Poyeshao$^n$ ('Orphan').

The boy grew to be a healthy, active little fellow. When he was old enough, his foster mother gave him a bow and arrows, and said "It is time for you to learn to hunt. To-morrow morning go to the woods and kill all the birds you can find."

Taking cobs of dry corn the woman shelled off the kernels and parched them in hot ashes; and the next morning she gave the boy some of the corn for his breakfast and rolled up some in a piece of buckskin and told him to take it with him, for he would be gone all day and would get hungry.

Poyeshao$^n$ started off and was very successful. At noon he sat down and rested and ate some of the parched corn, and then he hunted till the middle of the afternoon. When he began to work toward home he had a good string of birds.

The next morning Poyeshao$^n$'s foster mother gave him parched corn for breakfast and while he was eating she told him that he must do his best when hunting, for if he became a good hunter he would always be prosperous.

The boy took his bow and arrows and little bundle parched corn and went to the woods; again he found plenty of birds. At midday he ate his corn and thought over what his foster mother had told him. In his mind he said,

---

1 The story that opens this collection is taken from *Seneca Indian Myths* collected by Jeremiah Curtin, New York: E.P. Dutton & Company (1922), scanned at sacred-texts.com, July 2004 and redacted by John Bruno Hare. This text is in the public domain in the United States.

"I'll do just as my mother tells me, then some time I'll be able to hunt big game."

Poyeshao$^{n}$ hunted till toward evening, then went home with a larger string of birds than he had the previous day. His foster mother thanked him, and said, "Now you have begun to help me get food."

Early the next morning the boy's breakfast was ready and as soon as he had eaten it he took his little bundle of parched corn and started off. He went farther into the woods and at night came home with a larger string of birds than he had the second day. His foster mother praised and thanked him.

Each day the boy brought home more birds than the previous day. On the ninth day he killed so many that he brought them home on his back. His foster mother tied the birds in little bundles of three or four and distributed them among her neighbours.

The tenth day the boy started off, as usual and, as each day he had gone farther for game than on the preceding day, so now he went deeper into the woods than ever. About midday the sinew that held the feathers to his arrow loosened. Looking around for a place where he could sit down while he took the sinew off and wound it on again, he saw a small opening and near the centre of the opening a high, smooth, flat-topped, round stone. He went to the stone, sprang up on to it and sat down. He unwound the sinew and put it in his mouth to soften, then he arranged the arrow feathers and was about to fasten them to the arrow when a voice, right there near him, asked, "Shall I tell you stories?"

Poyeshao$^{n}$ looked up expecting to see a man, not seeing any one he looked behind the stone and around it, then he again began to tie the feathers to his arrow.

"Shall I tell you stories?" asked a voice right there by him.

The boy looked in every direction, but saw no one. Then he made up his mind to watch and find out who was trying to fool him. He stopped work and listened and when the voice again asked, "Shall I tell you stories?" he found that it came from the stone, then he asked, "What is that? What does it mean to tell stories?"

"It is telling what happened a long time ago. If you will give me your birds, I'll tell you stories."

"You may have the birds."

As soon as the boy promised to give the birds, the stone began telling what happened long ago. When one story was told, another was begun. The boy sat, with his head down, and listened. Toward night the stone said, "We will rest now. Come again to-morrow. If anyone asks about your birds, say that you have killed so many that they are getting scarce and you have to go a long way to find one."

While going home the boy killed five or six birds. When his foster mother asked why he had so few birds, he said that they were scarce; that he had to go far for them.

The next morning Poyeshao$^n$ started off with his bow and arrows and little bundle of parched corn, but he forgot to hunt for birds, he was thinking of the stories the stone had told him. When a bird lighted near him he shot it, but he kept straight on toward the opening in the woods. When he got there he put his birds on the stone, and called out, "I've come! Here are birds. Now tell me stories."

The stone told story after story. Toward night it said "Now we must rest till to-morrow."

On the way home the boy looked for birds, but it was late and he found only a few.

That night the foster mother told her neighbours that when Poyeshao$^n$ first began to hunt he had brought home a great many birds, but now he brought only four or five after being in the woods from morning till night. She said there was something strange about it, either he threw the birds away or gave them to some animal, or maybe he idled time away, didn't hunt. She hired a boy to follow Poyeshao$^n$ and find out what he was doing.

The next morning the boy took his bow and arrows and followed Poyeshao$^n$, keeping out of his sight and sometimes shooting a bird. Poyeshao$^n$ killed a good many birds; then, about the middle of the forenoon, he suddenly started off toward the east, running as fast as he could. The boy followed till he came to an opening in the woods and saw Poyeshao$^n$ climb up and sit down on a large round stone; he crept nearer and heard talking. When he couldn't see the person to whom Poyeshao$^n$ was talking he went up to the boy, and asked, "What are you doing here?"

"Hearing stories."

"What are stories?"

"Telling about things that happened long ago. Put your birds on this stone, and say, 'I've come to hear stories.'"

The boy did as told and straightway the stone began. The boys listened till the sun went down, then the stone said, "We will rest now. Come again to-morrow."

On the way home Poyeshao$^n$ killed three or four birds.

When the woman asked the boy she had sent why Poyeshao$^n$ killed so few birds, he said, "I followed him for a while, then I spoke to him, and after that we hunted together till it was time to come home. We couldn't find many birds."

The next morning the elder boy said, "I'm going with Poyeshao$^n$ to hunt, it's sport." The two started off together. By the middle of the forenoon each boy had a long string of birds. They hurried to the opening, put the birds on the stone, and said, "We have come, here are the birds! Tell us stories."

They sat on the stone and listened to stories till late in the afternoon, then the stone said, "We'll rest now till to-morrow."

On the way home the boys shot every bird they could find, but it was late and they didn't find many.

Several days went by in this way, then the foster mother said, "Those boys kill more birds than they bring home," and she hired two men to follow them.

The next morning, when Poyeshao$^n$ and his friend started for the woods the two men followed. When the boys had a large number of birds they stopped hunting and hurried to the opening. The men followed and, hiding behind trees, saw them put the birds on a large round stone, then jump up and sit there, with their heads down, listening to a man's voice; every little while they said, "*Û$^n$!*"

"Let's go there and find out who is talking to those boys," said one man to the other. They walked quickly to the stone, and asked, "What are you doing, boys?"

The boys were startled, but Poyeshao$^n$ said, "You must promise not to tell anyone."

They promised, then Poyeshao$^n$ said, "Jump up and sit on the stone."

The men seated themselves on the stone, then the boy said, "Go on with the story, we are listening."

The four sat with their heads down and the stone began to tell stories. When it was almost night the stone said, "To-morrow all the people in your village must come and listen to my stories. Tell the chief to send every man, and have each man bring something to eat. You must clean the brush away so the people can sit on the ground near me."

That night Poyeshao$^n$ told the chief about the storytelling stone, and gave him the stone's message. The chief sent a runner to give the message to each family in the village.

Early the next morning every one in the village was ready to start. Poyeshao$^n$ went ahead and the crowd followed. When they came to the opening each man put what he had brought, meat or bread, on the stone; the brush was cleared away, and every one sat down.

When all was quiet the stone said, "Now I will tell you stories of what happened long ago. There was a world before this. The things that I am going to tell about happened in that world. Some of you will remember every word that I say, some will remember a part of the words, and some will forget them all - I think this will be the way, but each man must do the best he can. Hereafter you must tell these stories to one another - now listen."

Each man bent his head and listened to every word the stone said. Once in a while the boys said "*Û$^n$!*" When the sun was almost down the stone said, "We'll rest now. Come tomorrow and bring meat and bread."

The next morning when the people gathered around the stone they found that the meat and bread they had left there the day before was gone. They put the food they had brought on the stone, then sat in a circle and waited. When all was quiet the stone began. Again it told stories till the sun was almost down, then it said, "Come tomorrow. Tomorrow I will finish the stories of what happened long ago.

Early in the morning the people of the village gathered around the stone and, when all was quiet, the stone began to tell stories, and it told till late in the afternoon, then it said, "I have finished! You must keep these stories as long as the world lasts; tell them to your children and grandchildren generation after generation. One person will remember them better than another. When you go to a man or a woman to ask for one of these stories, carry something to pay for it, bread or meat, or whatever you have. I know all that happened in the world before this; I have told it to you. When you visit one another, you must tell these things, and keep them up always. I have finished."

And so it has been. From the stone came all the knowledge the Senecas have of the world before this.

So the next time you sit down by a stone, stop and listen and you can access this knowledge too, for it is available to each and every one of us if only we are prepared to open our ears.

# Chapter 2
# BEGINNINGS AND ENDINGS

The reason why beginnings and endings are so important is that we remember more at the start and end of learning periods than in the middle as a result of the primacy and recency effects.

One suggested reason for the primacy effect is that the initial items presented are most effectively stored in long-term memory because of the greater amount of processing devoted to them. (The first list item can be rehearsed by itself; the second must be rehearsed along with the first, the third along with the first and second, and so on.) One suggested reason for the recency effect is that these items are still present in working memory when recall is required. As for the Items that benefit from neither effects, the middle items, these are the ones that are generally recalled most poorly.

Following on from this, it becomes evident that we should pay particular attention to the way we start and end our stories, presentations or lessons to ensure we make them effective and to achieve maximum possible impact.

When working with a large group, you might like to start with something like this:

*You all know my name by now but unfortunately I don't know yours, and I think it would be a good idea to change this. So, on the count of three, I'd like you all to do something for me please. On the count of three I'd like you all to shout out your first names please. Are you ready for it? Good, so here we go. One ... two ... three .... Fantastic! And now that we've been introduced, I'd like to tell you a story ...*

And here is a possible ending:

*Now please turn to the person you are sitting next to you and share something you feel you have learnt or benefited from as a result of attending this session.*

When it comes to storytelling, traditionally told tales often start with a few words at the beginning designed to prepare listeners for a different kind of discourse: a long narrative not supposed to be literally true, set in a kind of dreamtime that is apart from, but closely involved with, ordinary reality. The standard opening, the one that everyone knows, is "Once Upon a Time." However, there are many others to choose from. "There was, there was, and yet there was not", a personal favourite, is a popular way of introducing a story in the Caucasus, in both Georgia and Armenia. Here are some other options:

- At the time when men and animals were all the same and spoke the same language... (Traditional Navajo opening)

- I do not mean, I do not really mean that this story is true, but they say ... (Ashanti)

- In a certain kingdom, in a certain land, in a little village, there lived... (Russian)

- In a land that never was in a time that could never be...

- In ancient times, when the magpie was a Cossack chief and the duck a policeman, the bear had a long stumpy tail, as splendid as Mistress Fox's. (Tartar)

- In olden times, in times when rams were still without horns and sheep without tails, there lived... (Kazakh)

- In the days now long departed... (Scandinavian)

- In the old, old, half-forgotten times, before the gardens of Tartary were overrun with weeds, there lived ... (Tartar)

- It all happened long ago, and believe it or not, it is all absolutely true. (Traditional Irish opening)

- Long, long ago, soon after sky and earth had become separated so that there was room for trees to grow and the tribes of men to move between them, many gods and spirits still lived in the world. (Maori)

- Long, long ago, when some folk were already dead and others not yet born, there lived a ...(Tartar)
- Long, long ago, when there was less noise and more green on the broad banks of Lake Baikal, (Tartar)
- Long years ago, in the early ages of the world... (Hungarian)
- Many years ago, in a time when memory was young... (India)
- Once there was, one day there will be: this is the beginning of every fairy tale. There is no 'if' and no 'perhaps,' the three-legged stool unquestionably has three legs. (Breton)
- Once upon a time what happened did happen - and if it had not happened, you would never have heard this story. (Andrew Lang)
- Once upon a time, and a time before that ... (Scandinavian)
- So long ago that no one can quite say when ... (Scandinavian)
- This is my story which I have told you. If it be sweet, tell it to someone again and then some of the thanks will come back to me. (Africa)
- This is what the Old Ones told me when I was a child... (traditional Cherokee opening & ending)
- This tale goes back to a time long ago, when sheep grazed peacefully in the green folds of the Tartar homelands. (Tartar)
- ‘Twas not in my time, 'twas not in your time, but it was in somebody's time. (Irish)

Traditionally told stories often have formulaic endings too, to let listeners know the story is over, bring them back to earth, and ease the transition to normal conversation - or maybe whatever conversation is required in order to get the next tale started. The usual one is "and they all lived happily ever after." There are many alternatives though, some of which you can find listed below:

- And there happened in the end what should have happened in the beginning...and everyone knew and has never forgotten that whoever has a mind turned to wickedness is sure to end badly. (Andrew Lang)

- Chase the rooster and catch the hen, I'll never tell a lie like that again. (Bahamas)

- A grief shared by many is half a grief. A joy shared is twice a joy. (Vietnamese)

- I hope you won't fail to be pleased by my tale. For a potful of butter, I tell you another. (Russian)

- I jumped in the saddle and rode away to tell you the stories you've heard today. I jumped on a spoon and away I flew and you've heard all my stories, so God bless you. I jumped on a spindle and away I spun. And God bless me, my stories are done. (Romanian)

- If I get another story, I'll stick it behind your ears. (Ghana)

- If my story is not true, may the soles of my shoes turn to buttermilk. (Ireland)

- In that town there was a well and in that well there was a bell. And that is all I have to tell. (Russia)

- My story is done. Let some go and let some come! (Ghana)

- My story is done. But this story will go on, as long as grass grows and rivers run. (Native American)

- So you see, wonders abound...if you play your cards right. (Russian gypsy)

- They lived in peace, they died in peace, and there were buried in a pot of candle grease. (Bahamas)

- They reached a ripe old age and died in peace. (Russia)

- This is what the Old Ones told me when I was a child... (traditional Cherokee opening & ending)

- Three apples fell from heaven: one for the teller, one for the listener, and one for him (sic) who takes it to heart." (Armenian)

- We shall exist as long as our stories are moist with our breath. (Navajo saying)

- Well, whether it was false or true, the tale spread far and near, because the tale was fun to hear. (Saami)

- When the heart overflows, it comes out through the mouth. (Ethiopian)

- There is nothing to stop you and those you work with from being different, though, and finding your own ways to start and finish the stories you have to tell. In fact, the more original they are, the better, as this will no doubt help to make them more memorable too.

## Chapter 3
## THE STORY AS A JOURNEY

A story is, in a sense, a journey, as when you make a start on it, you do not necessarily know where you will be going, what will happen there, or who you are going to meet along the way. That explains our fascination with the form, and why, however many stories we hear or are told, we always want more and can never get enough of them.

As to why we choose to go on journeys, it could be to confirm or disprove our expectations about a place, or to find out something new about ourselves. And it is for these reasons we read stories too.

For stories in unfamiliar languages, as for journeys to unfamiliar places, extra preparations are clearly needed, and this is where the teacher or guide have a crucial role to play - in making the story or place more accessible to us, to ensure we are not deterred by what lies ahead and that we approach it in the right frame of mind. In a resource book notes for teachers can be provided to fulfil this requirement.

Another important point to make, and one that few would question, is that travelling can broaden the mind, and this applies not only to the physical journeys we undertake but also to the journeys we go on through stories - into the world of the imagination.

> See, your companions have gone;
> Will you not too make a start?
> If you desire to take wing as a bird,
> Then leave to the vultures this carrion world.
> Forsake your relations,
> For your real Friend must be sought ...

The lines above are taken from *The Secret Rose Garden* of Sa'd Ud Din Mahmud Shabistari, who was born in Persia, in Shabistar, near Tabriz, about 1250 CE. The work consists of a set of verses that uses the rich Sufi allegorical language to explore the path back to God, the Great Mystery, and the only journey some would say we ever truly take.

**Man Goes Walking**

A man goes walking, walking through a street market, with no particular aim in mind at the time, and is approached by a stall holder.

And the stall holder, what about the stall holder on this particular day? The stall holder is like a hunter stalking his prey.

"Come, buy one of my mirrors, buy one of my skilfully hand-crafted mirrors and treat yourself - a mirror with a difference, a mirror that shows you at your best, not with but without warts and all! And who could ever wish for more than that? There are some who would willingly give their right arms for such a chance!"

Man thinks about it and weighs up his options. Yes, but then again no … what is it that suits me myself I best? What would be best for me at this point in my life? Man decides and man responds.

"Tempting but the answer is no, my friend - a definite and resolute no I'm afraid. Your mirrors, tempting though they might be for many, are not for me."

How can that be? The streetwise stall holder asks. A never-to-be-repeated, once-in-a-lifetime offer and you turn down the chance? There are those who would merrily, and without hesitation, sell their souls to the devil for such a gift!

"Then more fools them!" The man responds. "What I want is a mirror I can step through, a mirror to lead me past my image in this world, an image I am only too familiar with, to the image of who I really am, and who I can really be.

And so the man carried on walking, and is still walking.

**Reference**

Shabistri, Sa'd Ud Din Mahmud (1920) *The Secret Rose Garden*, rendered from the Persian with an Introduction by Florence Lederer. London: J. Murray. Scanned, proofed and formatted at sacred-texts.com, September 2005, by John Bruno Hare. This text is in the public domain in the United States because it was published prior to 1923.

## Chapter 4
## TALES BUILT AROUND THE NUMBER THREE

Again and again in stories "*...we see how things appear in threes: how things have to happen three times, how the hero is given three wishes; how Cinderella goes to the ball three times; how the hero or the heroine is the third of three children.*" (Booker, 2004, p.229). But why does the triad, a group or series consisting of three items, feature over and over again in folktales and legends, wherever they may originate from? The answer is that it has long been of significance for a number of reasons, some of which are listed below:

- Photius, who was Patriarch of Constantinople from 858 to 867 and from 877 to 886, observed that the triad is the first odd number in energy, is the first perfect number and is a middle and analogy, and the Pythagoreans referred it to physiology, the cause of all that has the triple dimension. It was also believed to be the cause of good counsel, intelligence and knowledge, and a Mistress of Music, mistress also of Geometry, possessing authority in whatever pertains to astronomy and the nature and knowledge of the heavenly bodies, connecting and leading them into effects. Every virtue was also believed to be suspended from it, and to proceed from it. It was also known as a "Middle and Analogy," because all comparisons consist of three terms, at least; and analogies were called by the ancients "middles." Additionally, on account of the perfection of the triad, oracles were delivered from a tripod, as is related of the Oracle at Delphi.
- *Ezekiel xiv. v. 14* mentions three men who saw a creation, destruction and a restoration; Noah of the whole world, Daniel of the Jewish world Jerusalem and Job of his personal world.
- There is also the Hindu Trinity of Brahma, consisting of Brahma, Vishnu and Siva; Creator, Preserver and Changer.
- The Three Fates can be listed too - Clotho, Lachesis and Atropos. Then there are the Three Furies - Tisiphone, Alecto and Megæra.

Mention can also be made of the Three Graces - Euphrosyne, Aglaia and Thalia. In addition, there are the Three Judges of Hades - Minos, Æacus and Rhadamanthus.

- As for the Druids, their poems are noted as being composed in triads.
- Then there is the transcendent importance of the Christian Trinity. In old paintings we often see a trinity of Jesus with John and Mary.
- For the Jews, monograms of Jehovah were triple; thus three rays and the *Shin*, and three *yods* in a triangle.
- In the *Timæus* of Plato, the Divine Triad is called *Theos:* God; Logos, the Word and Psyche, the Soul. Indeed it is impossible to study any single system of worship throughout the world, without being struck by the peculiar persistence of the triple number in regard to divinity; whether as a group of deities, a triformed or three-headed god, a Mysterious Triunity, a deity of three powers, or a family relationship of three Persons, such as the Father, Mother and Son of the Egyptians, Osiris, Isis and Horus.
- Three is a notable number in the mythology of the Norseman too: the great Ash-tree Yggdrasil supported the world. It had three roots; one extended into Asgard, the abode of the Gods; one into Jotenheim, the home of the Giants, and the third into Nifleheim, the region of the Unknown. The three Norns (Fates) attend to the root in Asgard: they were Urda (the past); Verdandi (the present) and Skulda (the future).
- The *Talmuds* are crowded with quaint conceits concerning the triad, and many are very curious:- He who three times daily repeats the 114th Psalm is sure of future happiness; Three precious gifts were given to the Jews - the Law of Moses, the Land of Israel and Paradise; In three sorts of dreams there is truth; the last dream of the morning, the dream which is also dreamed by a neighbour, and a dream twice repeated; Three things calm a man; melody, scenery and sweet scent: and three things improve a man; a fine house, a handsome wife and good furniture; Three despise their fellows; cooks, fortune-tellers and dogs; Three love their fellows; proselytes, slaves and ravens; Three persons live a life which is no life; he who lives at another man's table, he who is ruled by his wife, and he who is incapable from bodily affliction.
- Then there are three keys which God keeps to himself, and which no man can gain nor use; the key of life, the key of rain and the

key of the resuscitation of the dead. *Taanith*, 2; 1 and 2; The Jewish butcher of Kosher meat must use three knives; one to slaughter the animal, another to cut it up and a third to remove the suet, which it is forbidden to eat; Three acolytes had to attend the High Priest when he went in to worship; one at his right, one at his left, and one had to hold up the gems on the train of his vestment.

- Among the Brahmins there were three great *Vedas*; three *Margas* or ways of salvation; three *Gunas*, the *Satva*, quiescence; *Rajas*, desire; and *Tamas*, decay. Three *Lokas* - *Swarga, Bhumi* and *Patala*; heaven, earth and hell. Three Jewels of wisdom, the *Tri-ratnas*; Buddha, *Dharma* and *Sanga*. The three Fires are the three aspects of the human soul - *Atma, Buddhi* and *Manas*. There were three prongs of the trident, and three eyes in the forehead of Siva. Note also the three-syllabled holy word *AUM*.
- At the Oblation of the Elements in the Celtic Church, three drops of wine and three drops of water were poured into the chalice. And in the present Christian Church we notice three crossings with water at Baptism, three Creeds, the Banns of Marriage are published three times and a Bishop in benediction makes the Sign of the Cross three times. In Roman Catholic churches, the Angelus Bell is rung three times a day, a peal of three times three for the heavenly hierarchies of angels: Pope John XXII ordered that the faithful should say three *Aves* on each occasion.
- Last but not least, mention should be made of the *I Ching* or *Book of Changes*, one of the oldest of the Chinese classic texts, as it contains a divination system based on triads. The standard text originated from the ancient text transmitted by Fei Zhi ( c50 BCE - CE 10) of the Han Dynasty. Each hexagram represents a description of a state or process and is composed of four three-line arrangements called *trigrams*, of which there are eight:— *khien, tui, li, chan, sien, khan, kan* and *kwan*; each expressed by figures of one long and two short lines. (Adapted from *The Triad* in Westcott, 1911, pp. 41-48).
- There is also The *Threefold Law* (a.k.a. the *Law of Return*) in the *Wiccan Rede*, an ethical code for witches, which adds a reward for those who follow the code, and a punishment for those who violate it. The law states that "All good that a person does to another returns three fold in this life; harm is also returned three fold."

Now for a triad of stories constructed around triads. The first is an old Jewish folktale, the second is a *Charles Perrault* story, and the third is one of my own:

**Three Precepts**

A hunter once caught a bird that was very clever and able to speak seventy languages, and it thus addressed its captor, "Set me free, and I will teach you three precepts which will be of great use to you."

"Tell me these rules, and I will set you free," said the fowler.

"Swear to me first," retorted the clever bird, "that you will keep your promise and in truth set me free."

And when the man swore to keep his promise, the bird said, "My first precept is: never rue anything that has happened. My second rule of conduct is: never believe anything you are told that is impossible and beyond belief. My third precept is: never try to reach something that is unattainable."

Having spoken thus, the bird reminded the bird-catcher of his promise and asked him to set him free, and the man opened his hand and let the captive bird fly away.

The bird sat down on the top of a tree that was taller than all the other trees, and mockingly called to the man below, "Stupid man, you did allow me to fly away not knowing that a precious pearl was hidden in my body, a pearl that is the cause of my great wisdom."

When the bird-catcher heard these words he greatly regretted having allowed the bird to fly away, and rushing up to the tree, he tried to climb it, but failing in his efforts he fell down and broke his legs.

The bird only laughed aloud, and said, "Stupid man! Not an hour has passed since I taught you three wise precepts, and you have already forgotten them. I told you never to rue anything that was past, and you did repent having set me free. I told you never to believe anything that was evidently beyond belief, and you were credulous enough to believe that I actually carried a costly pearl in my body. I am only a poor wild bird hourly in search of my nourishment. And finally, I advised you never to strive in vain after the unattainable, while you did try to catch a bird with your hands, and are now lying below with broken legs. It is of men of your kidney that the philosopher has said, 'A reproof entereth more into a wise man than an hundred stripes into a fool.' (*Proverbs, Ch. 17, v. 10*). But alas, you are no exception, for there are many men as unwise as yourself."

And thus speaking, the wise bird flew away in search of nourishment.

**The Ridiculous Wishes**

There was once a poor woodcutter who, tired of his hard life, longed for rest in the world to come. In his unhappiness, he declared that in all his days, heaven had not granted even one of his wishes.

One day in the woods, as the woodcutter was complaining of his unhappy lot, Jupiter appeared before him, his thunderbolts in his hands. It would be difficult to picture the terror of the poor man.

"I desire nothing," he said, casting himself on the ground. I will give up my wishes if you, in turn, will give up your thunder. That's a fair exchange!"

"Have no fear," said Jupiter. "I have heard your complaints and I have come to show you how unfairly you judge me. Now listen! I am king of all the world and I promise to grant your first three wishes, no matter what they may be. See that they make you happy and content; and since your happiness depends on them, think carefully before you make them."

With these words, Jupiter returned to his heavens and the happy woodcutter, taking up his bundle of sticks, hurried to his home. Never had his burden seemed so light.

"This is an important matter," he said to himself. ''I certainly must have my wife's advice."

"Hey, Fanchon," he shouted, as he entered his cottage. "Let us up a good fire. We are rich for the rest of our lives. All we have to do is to make three wishes!"

With this, he told his wife what had happened, whereupon she in her imagination began to form a thousand plans. But realizing the importance of acting prudently, she said to her husband, "Blaise, my dear, let us not spoil anything by our impatience. We must think things over very carefully. Let us put off our first wish until tomorrow. Let us sleep on it."

"I think you are right," said he, "but first go draw some of that special wine."

On her return, the woodcutter drank deeply and leaned back in his chair before the fire. "To match such a fine blaze," he said, "I wish we had a measure of sausage. It would go very well indeed!"

Scarcely had he spoken these words when his wife, to her great astonishment, saw a long link of sausage moving over to them like a snake from the chimney corner. She cried out in alarm, but realizing at once that this was the result of the wish which her foolish husband had made, she began to abuse and scold him angrily.

"When you might," she said, "have a kingdom, with gold, pearls, rubies, diamonds, fine clothes; and all you wish for is a sausage!"

"Alas," her husband replied. "I was wrong, I made a very bad choice. I admit my mistake. Next time I will do better."

"Yes! Yes!" said his wife. "I'll repeat it till Doomsday. To make such a choice as you did, you must be a donkey."

At this the husband became very angry and almost wished his wife was dead. "Mankind," he said, "is born to suffer. A curse on this and all sausages. I wish that it was hanging from the end of your nose!"

The wish was heard at once in heaven, and the sausage fastened itself on her nose. Fanchon had once been pretty, and - to tell the truth - this ornament did not have a very pleasing effect. Since it hung down over her face, however, it interfered with her talking, and this was such an advantage to her husband that he did not think he had wished too badly.

"With my remaining wish I could very well still make myself a king," he said to himself. "But we must think of the queen, too, and her unhappiness if she were to sit on the throne with her new yard-long nose. She must decide which she wants, to be a queen with that nose or a woodcutter's wife and an ordinary person."

Whereupon his wife agreed that they had no choice. She would never have the riches and diamonds and fine clothes she had dreamed of, but she would be herself again if the last wish would free her from the frightful sausage on her nose.

And so the woodcutter did not change his lot. He did not become a king. His purse was not filled with gold. He was only too glad to use his remaining wish in restoring his poor wife to her former state.

**The Three Bees**

This is the story of three unfortunate bees whose curiosity got the better of them one sunny day when they fell into an open jam jar.

The first bee wasn't particularly concerned about his predicament because his partner had always rescued him from tricky situations in the past and he trusted that she would do so again. In fact, he'd grown to depend on her. So he just sat back in the jam and waited because he knew that he'd be all right. What happened to him? He died waiting.

The second bee kept climbing the slippery glass wall until he reached the rounded rim, then fell back down again. And the more times he fell, the more determined it made him. He was a fighter and he refused to give in. What happened to him? He died of exhaustion.

The third bee was different to the others and had never really fitted into the hive. In fact, he'd become a social outcast and lived a very solitary life. The other bees had found him to be rather strange and refused to have anything to do with him. Anyway, while his colleagues were otherwise occupied with their attempts to escape, he chose to taste the jam and what do you know? He found he really liked it. So he ate and he ate and he ate until he'd licked the jar clean. And what happened to him? Well he died too, but he died of pleasure.

**Bibliography**

Ashliman, D.L. Folklore and Mythology Electronic Texts www.pitt.edu/~dash/folktexts.html (accessed 27/09/09)

Berman, M. (2010) *All God's Creatures*, California: Pendraig Publshing.

Booker, C. (2004) *The Seven Basic Plots: Why we tell Stories*, London: Continuum.

Perrault, C. (1921) *Old-Time Stories told by Master Charles Perrault*, translated by A. E. Johnson, New York: Dodd Mead and Company.

Rappoport, A.S. (1937) *The Folklore of the Jews*, London: The Soncino Press, 1937. No copyright notice.

Westcott, W.W. (1911) (3rd Edition) *Numbers, Their Occult Power and Mystic Virtues*, London, Benares: Theosophical Pub. Society. Scanned, proofed and formatted at sacred-texts.com, August 2009, by John Bruno Hare. This text is in the public domain in the US because it was published prior to 1923.

## Chapter 5
## TEACHING TALES FROM THE SUFI & HASIDIC TRADITIONS

Teaching tales have a long and honoured history for being a way to entertain and, at the same time, educate people. The earliest examples were probably chants or songs of praise for the natural world in Pagan times. And since stories first began being told, one of the methods of passing on a culture's teaching has involved a student sitting at his teacher's feet and listening to the tales that teacher had to tell of times and people gone by. The stories of early India, the Greek fables, Taoist, Zen, Sufi and Hasidic tales are all examples of trying to pass on not just a cultural tale but a valuable lesson as well.

The author and Jesuit priest Anthony de Mello tells of a master who always gave his teachings in parables and stories, much to the frustration of his disciples who wanted straightforward answers to their questions. To their objections the master would answer, "You have yet to understand my dears, that the shortest distance between truth and a human being is a story."

Wisdom tales can remind us of higher goals, and provide the inspiration to practise what we know on a daily basis. Spiritual and cultural traditions the world round have provided tales of how others have danced and stumbled along life's path for this very purpose. Stories offer us doorways into new ways of seeing and being in the world. The secret is that the story door opens inward. When we draw the stories deeply into our imaginations, and make connections from them to our own lives, they become a part of us, like a wise advisor ready to remind us of another way of seeing and responding to life. The shortest tales are especially good for this purpose as they are easily learned and shared spontaneously. It is not always possible to take the time to spin out an elaborate yarn to make a point and we are often called to offer stories in non-performance settings - responding to an immediate issue - with friends, or family or colleagues.

Author, and storyteller Clarrissa Pinkola Estes, described the phenomenon of story living in our psyches as 'medicine' that serves us when we need it. This can happen just by hearing a tale. But for a story to be readily available to us, we often must help it to sink in, so that its imagery makes connections in our hearts, memories and imaginations, allowing new learning to arise.

Anthony de Mello (1986) suggests in the introduction to his collection *One-Minute Wisdom*, that we "take one story at a time." Perhaps it would be a good idea to take his advice one step further and to read not more than one story per week. The hunger for the good story, and for spiritual inspiration, often drives us to plough through story collections like children in a sweetshop. We read one after the other, tasting the unique flavour of each, enough to say, "Mmm, I like that one, or so-so," often bypassing altogether those that have already been tried. This way of tasting stories is like reading a description of the story on its door, rather than opening the door to be deeply touched by the tale. This is the way of our consumerist culture, but stories call us to be with them in a more time-honoured way.

The tales presented here are examples from the Hasidic tradition and the first three all have something to do with water. Sometimes a stretch of water can act as a barrier or a source of division, especially when the people involved in the matter have tunnel vision and walk around wearing blinkers over their eyes! Khelm in Yiddish folklore is the equivalent of Gotham in British tales - the place where stupid people are supposed to live:

**A Bridge in Khelm**

A river flowed right through the middle of Khelm. It occurred to several merchants that a bridge over it would be good for business on both sides of the river. But some of the younger people objected. They said, "Of course it would be nice to build a bridge, but let's not do it because it would be good for business; we should build it solely for aesthetic reasons. We'd be glad to contribute towards the cost for beauty's sake, but we won't give a penny for the sake of trade."

Still others, even younger people, said, "A bridge! That's a good idea, but not for the sake of trade or beauty but to have some place to stroll back and forth. We'd be glad to contribute money to build a bridge for strolling, but not for any other reason."

And so the three groups began to quarrel, and they are quarrelling still. And to the present day Khelm still does not have a bridge.

**Water Wouldn't Hurt**

An exhausted disciple came running to his Holy Man.

"Teacher, help. Take pity. My house is burning."

The Holy Man calmed his disciple. Then, fetching his staff from a corner of the room, he said, "Here, take my staff. Run back to your house. Draw circles around it with my staff, each circle some seven handbreadths from the other. At the seventh circle, step back seven handbreadths, then lay my staff down at the east end of the fire."

The disciple hurriedly noted the instructions down, grabbed the staff and started off.

"Listen," the Holy Man called after him, "on second thoughts, it wouldn't hurt also to pour on water. Yes, in God's name, pour on water. As much water as you bloody well can!"

**Blood and Water**

Once upon a time there was a king who went to a river to bathe. When he came to its bank, he saw that half of the stream was water but the other half was blood. And there was a man in the middle trying to cross over from the blood to the water.

The king was puzzled by this so he called together all the priests, rabbis and other holy folk to ask them what it meant. But none of them could see anything in the river but water and they could only come to the conclusion that the King was seeing things and that perhaps he was suffering from stress.

But the king was not convinced. So he sent for the greatest rabbi in the city, and this rabbi saw exactly what the King had seen. And this was his interpretation:

"Half of the river is the blood that has been spilled," said the rabbi, "And the other half is the tears that Jews have wept. The man in the middle is your father, who is trying to cross from hell into paradise. But to do this he must wade out of the Jewish blood he has shed, and the river will not let him."

*The next two tales feature elflike creatures from Yiddish folklore - the* shretele *and the* kapelyushniklekh. *For magic to work, faith in the process is required. This seems to be a quality we come into the world with but it somehow gets lost along the way. The great-grandfather of the narrator in the following tale had clearly lost his. But what about you?*

**The Passover Elf Helps Great-Grandmother**

One Saturday evening in fall, after the holidays, my great-grandmother was standing beside the stove rendering down goose fat. She was all alone in the kitchen; the house was hushed and still. Suddenly in the chimney corner, she saw a tiny hand stretched out, palm up, as if it were asking for something. She felt terribly frightened but forced herself to remain calm while she put a piece of crackling into the little hand. The she started to pour the rendered fat from the frying pan into containers. But no matter how often she poured from the pan, it stayed full. She poured and poured until every vessel in the house was brimming with fat. Every pot, every pitcher, every tub. And the fat continued to flow as from a spring.

About midnight my great-grandfather woke up and saw that the kitchen was brightly lighted and his wife was still standing at the stove. He got out of bed and said irritably, "Why are you fussing with that fat at this hour? It's almost dawn."

"Well," said my great-grandmother, "there went that. Too bad. Our household was being blessed: we had an elf, a shretele, in the house, and now you've chased it away."

*Instead of being victims, we can take responsibility for what happens to us. The question that forms the title of the next tale could be replaced by the following: "Who's in control of your life?"*

**Who's Milking the Cows?**

There was a dairyman who had several cows that gave a great deal of milk. When they suddenly went dry, he realized that someone must be milking them. He watched them carefully all day but saw no one, yet when he tried to milk them the next morning, he couldn't get even a glassful from them. That night at nine o' clock, the man went into the cow barn. He lighted a candle and set it under a great barrel, hid himself in a corner, and settled down for the night. At two in the morning he heard footsteps; then a tiny man and a tiny woman came into the barn. They both wore little caps, and the woman's hair was braided and tied with pretty ribbons. He watched as they seated themselves on milking stools, set buckets under the cows, and started in to milk. At that the man upended the barrel, and when his candle lit up the barn the kapelyushniklekh, the little cap-wearers, started running. The male got away, but the dairyman was able to catch the female, and he beat her severely. She pleaded with him, saying, "If you spare my life we'll never come back, and your cows will give you double the amount of milk they used to."

And that's exactly what happened.

*Now for some examples from the Sufi tradition. For many of us life is spent searching for something that we never seem able to find. The reason for this can perhaps be found in the following tale:*

**The Key**

A drunk is searching the ground under a street lamp. A friend sees him there and asks him what he is doing. The drunk slurs, "I'm looking for my key."

The friend helps him search everywhere. Half an hour later they still have not found the key. The friend asks, "Are you sure you lost it here?"

"No," replies the drunk, "I lost it inside my house."

"Then why are you looking here?"

"Because the light is here."

*Some of us develop the art of lying to such an extent that we eventually end up not only deceiving others but ourselves as well. That's perhaps what the following tale is all about:*

**Free Bread**

The Mullah's wife sent him to buy some bread. When the Mullah arrived at the bread shop he saw a long line waiting to buy bread. He thought he would do something to get in front of the line. He shouted, "People, don't you know the Sultan's daughter is getting married tonight and he is giving away free bread?"

The multitude ran toward the palace as the Sultan was generous to a fault and loved his daughter more than anyone. The Mullah was now in front of the line and was about to buy his bread when he thought to himself, "Mullah, you are truly a fool. All the citizen's are getting free bread tonight and I am about to pay for it." So he ran to the palace and when he got there was thoroughly beaten by the disappointed people.

*They say that God works in mysterious ways and the following tale reinforces that message:*

**Who Knows?**

Many years ago a wise peasant lived in China. He had a son who was the gleam in his eyes and a white stallion that was his favourite belonging. One day his horse escaped from his grounds and disappeared into the fields outside the village. The villagers came to him one by one and announced their condolences. They said, "You are such an unlucky man. It is so bad."

The peasant answered, "Who knows. Maybe it's bad, maybe it's good." The populace left. The next day the stallion returned followed by twelve wild horses. The same people returned and told our wise man about how lucky he was.

"It's so good."

He replied once more, "Who knows. Maybe it's good, maybe it's bad."

As it happens, the next day his one and only son was attempting to break in one of the wild horses when the horse fell down and broke his leg. Once more everyone came to condole with him. They said, "It's so bad."

Again he replied, "Who knows. Maybe it's bad, maybe it's good." Three days passed and his poor son was limping around the village with his broken leg, when the emperor's army entered the village announcing that a war was starting and they conscripted all the young men of the village. However, they left the son since he had a broken leg. Once more, everyone was so jealous of our man. They surrounded him talking about his amazing luck.

"It is so good for you," they said. He answered all thus,

"Who knows. Maybe it's good, maybe it's bad."

*Nasrudin Hodja is perhaps Islam's best-known trickster. His legendary wit and trickery were possibly based on the exploits and words of a historical imam. Nasrudin was reputedly born in 1208 in the village of Horto near Sivrihisar. In 1237 he moved to Aksehir, where he died in the Islamic year 683 (1284 or 1285). As many as three hundred and fifty anecdotes have been attributed to the* Hodja, *as he is called. Hodja is a title meaning teacher or scholar.*

*An element of truth can be found in every assertion ever made so nothing should ever be dismissed out of hand. The following Nasrudin tale can be used to illustrate this:*

**Everyone is Right**

Once when Nasrudin Hodja was serving as a magistrate, one of his neighbours came to him with a complaint against a fellow neighbour.

Nasrudin listened to the charges carefully, then concluded, "Yes, dear neighbour, you're quite right."

Then the other neighbour came to him. The magistrate listened to his defence carefully, then concluded, "Yes, dear neighbour, you're quite right."

Nasrudin's wife, having listened in on the entire proceedings, said to him, "Husband, both men cannot be right."

The magistrate answered, "Yes, dear wife, you're quite right."

*One of my problems is that I can never remember the names of people I don't like, which is probably why the next tale appeals to me:*

**The Wife's Name**

Nasrudin Hodja and a friend were discussing their wives, when it occurred to the friend that Nasrudin had never mentioned his wife's name.

"What is your wife's name?" he asked.

"I do not know her name," admitted the Hodja.

"What?" asked the friend in disbelief. "How long have you been married?"

"Twenty years," answered the Hodja, then added, "At first I did not think that the marriage would last, so I did not take the effort to learn my bride's name."

*Fine theories are all very well but they are not going to sustain you in the way that food and drink will. Our survival ultimately depends on more practical considerations as can be seen from the following tale that concludes this section:*

**The Recipe**

The Hodja purchased a piece of meat at the market, and on his way home he met a friend. Seeing the Hodja's purchase, the friend told him an excellent recipe for stew.

"I'll forget it for sure," said the Hodja. "Write it on a piece of paper for me."

The friend obliged him, and the Hodja continued on his way, the piece of meat in one hand and the recipe in the other. He had not walked far when suddenly a large hawk swooped down from the sky, snatched the meat, and flew away with it.

"It will do you no good!" shouted the Hodja after the disappearing hawk. "I still have the recipe!"

## Chapter 6

## TALES BUILT AROUND THE NUMBER SEVEN

The Heptad, a group or series consisting of seven items, has long been of significance for all sorts of reasons. First of all, let us consider the human body:—

- The body has seven obvious parts - the head, chest, abdomen, two legs and two arms. There are seven internal organs - stomach, liver, heart, lungs, spleen and two kidneys. The ruling part, the head, has seven parts for external use - two eyes, two ears, two nostrils and a mouth. There are seven inflections of the voice - the acute, grave, circumflex, rough, smooth, the long and the short sounds. The hand makes seven motions - up and down, to the right and left, before and behind, and circular. There are seven evacuations - tears from the eyes, mucus of the nostrils, the saliva, the semen, two excretions and the perspiration. (We could also add that it is in the seventh month the human offspring becomes viable and that menstruation tends to occur in series of four times seven days).
- As to the sacredness of the number seven, among the Hebrews oaths were confirmed by seven witnesses or by seven victims offered in sacrifice (cf. the covenant between Abraham and Abimelech with seven lambs, *Genesis*, chap. xxi. vv. 28, 21-28). The Persian Sun God, Mithras, had the number seven sacred to him too.
- The highest beings in Zoroastrianism, the Amshaspands, are also seven in number: Ormuzd, source of life; Bahman, the king of this world; Ardibehest, fire producer; Shahrivar, the former of metals; Spandarmat, queen of the earth (the Gnostic Sophia); Khordad, the ruler of times and seasons and Amerdad, ruling over the vegetable world.
- Sanskrit lore has very frequent references to the number seven too: *Sapta Rishi,* seven sages; *Sapta Kula*, seven castes; *Sapta Loka*, seven

worlds; *Sapta Para,* seven cities; *Sapta Dwipa,* seven holy islands; *Sapta Arania,* seven deserts; *Sapta Parna,* seven human principles; *Sapta Samudra*, seven holy seas and *Sapta Vruksha,* seven holy trees.

- The Assyrian Tablets also teem with groups of sevens: seven gods of sky; seven gods of earth; seven gods of fiery spheres; seven gods maleficent; seven phantoms; spirits of seven heavens and spirits of seven earths.
- The Moon passes through stages of seven days in increase, full, decrease, and renewal, and there are the seven stars in the head of Taurus called the Pleiades.
- The Kabalists describe seven classes of Angels: Ishim, Arelim, Chashmalim, Melakim, Auphanim, Seraphim and Kerubim. The Judaic Hell was given seven names by the Kabalists too: Sheol, Abaddon, Tihahion, Bar Shacheth, Tzelmuth, Shaari Muth and Gehinnom.
- Other heptads can be added to those above too. The seven prophetesses in the *Old Testament* are Sarah, Miriam, Deborah, Hannah, Abigail, Huldah and Esther. The seven Catholic Deadly Sins are pride, covetousness, lust, anger, gluttony, envy and sloth. The seven Gifts of the Holy Spirit (*Isaiah* xi. v. 2) are wisdom, understanding, counsel, fortitude, knowledge, piety and fear of the Lord. The seven Champions of Christendom were St. George for England, St. Denis of France, St. James of Spain, St. Andrew of Scotland, St. David of Wales, St. Patrick of Ireland and St. Antonio of Italy.
- We can also add the historic city of Rome to the list, which was built upon Seven Hills; the Palatine, Cœlian, Aventine, Viminal, Quirinal, Esquiline and the Capitol (adapted from *The Heptad* in Westcott, 1911, pp. 72-84).
- Last but not least, mention should be made of what have been described as the seven basic plots (see Booker, 2004), and the suggestion that all the stories that have ever been written are based on these. The seven basic plot types Christopher Booker identifies are overcoming the monster, rags to riches, the quest, voyage and return, comedy, tragedy and rebirth.

*Now for some examples of stories built around the number seven. The first is a German tale, the second from Norway and the third from the Philippines:*

**The Seven Steps**

On the main road from Nenndorf to Hannover in the vicinity of the village of Eberloh, right next to the road, there can be seen seven upright stones spaced like footsteps. They have been carefully preserved even to this day. They are called the seven steps, and the following legend is associated with them:

Many years ago two peasants came into conflict about the boundary between their adjoining fields. The one accused the other of ploughing away some of his land. The accused man swore with an oath that he was innocent. Later the accuser wanted to prove that his neighbour had perjured himself, and invited the court to see the fields for themselves.

The person who had sworn the oath appeared as well, and said, "If I have sworn falsely then may God grant that I take no more than seven steps." With his seventh step he disappeared, and was never seen again.

**The Seventh Father of the House**

Once upon a time there was a man who was travelling about, and he came at length to a big and fine farm. There was such a fine manor house there that it might well have been a little castle.

"It would be a nice thing to get a night's rest here," said the man to himself, upon entering the gate. Close by stood an old man with gray hair and beard, chopping wood.

"Good evening, father," said the traveller. "Can I get lodgings here tonight?"

"I am not the father of the house," said the old man. "Go into the kitchen and speak to my father!" The traveller went into the kitchen. There he met a man who was still older, and he was lying on his knees in front of the hearth, blowing into the fire.

"Good evening, father. Can I get lodgings here tonight?" asked the traveller.

"I am not the father of the house," said the old man. "But go in and speak to my father. He is sitting at the table in the parlour."

So the traveller went into the parlour and spoke to him who was sitting at the table. He was much older than the other two, and he sat there with chattering teeth, shaking, and reading in a big book, almost like a little child.

"Good evening, father. Can you give me lodgings here tonight?" said the man.

"I am not the father of the house. But speak to my father over there. He is sitting on the bench," said the man who was sitting at the table with chattering teeth, and shaking and shivering. So the traveller went to him who was sitting on the bench. He was getting a pipe of tobacco ready, but he was so bent with age, and his hands shook so much, that he was scarcely able to hold the pipe.

"Good evening, father," said the traveller again. "Can I get lodgings here tonight?"

"I am not the father of the house," said the old, bent-over man. "But speak to my father, who is in the bed over yonder."

The traveller went to the bed, and there lay an old, old man, and the only thing about him that seemed to be alive was a pair of big eyes.

"Good evening, father. Can I get lodgings here tonight?" said the traveller.

"I am not the father of the house. But speak to my father, who lies in the cradle yonder," said the man with the big eyes. Yes, the traveller went to the cradle. There was a very old man lying, so shrivelled up, that he was not larger than a baby, and one could not have told that there was life in him if it had not been for a sound in his throat now and then.

"Good evening, father. Can I get lodgings here tonight?" said the man. It took some time before he got an answer, and still longer before he had finished it. He said, like the others, that he was not the father of the house. "But speak to my father. He is hanging up in the horn on the wall there."

The traveller stared around the walls, and at last he caught sight of the horn. But when he looked for him who hung in it, there was scarcely anything to be seen but a lump of white ashes, which had the appearance of a man's face. Then he was so frightened, that he cried aloud, "Good evening, father. Will you give me lodgings here tonight?"

There was a sound like a little tomtit's chirping, and he was barely able to understand that it meant, "Yes, my child."

And now a table came in which was covered with the costliest dishes, with ale and brandy. And when he had eaten and drunk, in came a good bed with reindeer skins, and the traveller was very glad indeed that he at last had found the true father of the house.

**The Seven Crazy Fellows**

Once there were living in the country in the northern part of Luzon seven crazy fellows, named Juan, Felipe, Mateo, Pedro, Francisco, Eulalio, and Jacinto. They were happy all the day long.

One morning Felipe asked his friends to go fishing. They stayed at the Cagayan River a long time. About two o'clock in the afternoon Mateo said to his companions, "We are hungry; let us go home!"

"Before we go," said Juan, "let us count ourselves, to see that we are all here!"

He counted; but because he forgot to count himself, he found that they were only six, and said that one of them had been drowned. Thereupon they all dived into the river to look for their lost companion; and when they came out, Francisco counted to see if he had been found; but he, too, left himself out, so in they dived again.

Jacinto said that they should not go home until they had found the one who was lost. While they were diving, an old man passed by. He asked the fools what they were diving for. They said that one of them had been drowned.

"How many were you at first?" said the old man.

They said that they were seven.

"All right," said the old man. "Dive in, and I will count you."

They dived, and he found that they were seven. Since he had found their lost companion, he asked them to come with him.

When they reached the old man's house, he selected Mateo and Francisco to look after his old wife; Eulalio he chose to be water carrier; Pedro, cook; Jacinto, wood carrier and Juan and Felipe, his companions in hunting.

When the next day came, the old man said that he was going hunting, and he told Juan and Felipe to bring along rice with them. In a little while they reached the mountains, and he told the two fools to cook the rice at ten o'clock. He then went up the mountain with his dogs to catch a deer. Now, his two companions, who had been left at the foot of the mountain, had never seen a deer. When Felipe saw a deer standing under a tree, he thought that the antlers of the deer were the branches of a small tree without leaves: so he hung his hat and bag of rice on them, but the deer immediately ran away.

When the old man came back, he asked if the rice was ready. Felipe told him that he had hung his hat and the rice on a tree that ran away.

The old man was angry, and said, "That tree you saw was the antlers of a deer. We'll have to go home now, for we have nothing to eat."

Meanwhile the five crazy fellows who had been left at home were not idle. Eulalio went to get a pail of water. When he reached the well and saw his image in the water, he nodded, and the reflection nodded back at him. He did this over and over again; until finally, becoming tired, he jumped into the water, and was drowned.

Jacinto was sent to gather small sticks, but he only destroyed the fence around the garden.

Pedro cooked a chicken without removing the feathers. He also let the chicken burn until it was as black as coal.

Mateo and Francisco tried to keep the flies off the face of their old mistress. They soon became tired, because the flies kept coming back; so they took big sticks to kill them with. When a fly lighted on the nose of the old woman, they struck at it so hard that they killed her. She died with seemingly a smile on her face. The two fools said to each other that the old woman was very much pleased that they had killed the fly.

When the old man and his two companions reached home, the old man asked Pedro if there was any food to eat. Pedro said that it was in the pot. The old man looked in and saw the charred chicken and feathers. He was very angry at the cook.

Then he went in to see his wife, and found her dead. He asked Mateo and Francisco what they had done to the old woman. They said that they had only been killing flies that tried to trouble her, and that she was very much pleased by their work.

The next thing the crazy fellows had to do was to make a coffin for the dead woman; but they made it flat, and in such a way that there was nothing to prevent the corpse from falling off. The old man told them to carry the body to the church but on their way they ran, and the body rolled off the flat coffin. They said to each other that running was a good thing, for it made their burden lighter.

When the priest found that the corpse was missing, he told the six crazy fellows to go back and get the body. While they were walking toward the house, they saw an old woman picking up sticks by the roadside.

"Old woman, what are you doing here?" they said. "The priest wants to see you."

While they were binding her, she cried out to her husband, "Ah! Here are some bad boys trying to take me to the church."

But her husband said that the crazy fellows were only trying to tease her. When they reached the church with this old woman, the priest, who was also crazy, performed the burial ceremony over her. She cried out that she was alive; but the priest answered that since he had her burial fee, he did not care whether she was alive or not. So they buried this old woman in the ground.

When they were returning home, they saw the corpse that had fallen from the coffin on their way to the church. Francisco cried that it was the ghost of the old woman. Terribly frightened, they ran away in different directions, and became scattered all over Luzon.

*The final example is an etiological tale. These days people pick up partners in pubs or clubs, but there was a time when the pick-up place might well have been a brook or a well where people would have gone to draw water. And that's how girl meets boy in the story from Armenia that follows:*

**The Seven Stars**

There were once six brothers, the youngest of which was a very handsome youth. One day he went hunting and fell asleep by a brook. A beautiful girl had been sent by her mother to the brook for water. There she saw the handsome boy and fell in love with him. The boy woke up and, seeing her, fell in love with her. "Let's go away together and get married and set up our own house," the boy said.

"Fine," said the girl, "but let me take this water back to my family first."

So the girl took the water home and told her family that she was going to marry the boy at the brook and that, together, they were going away. The family, seeing that the girl was in love, knew that she could not be discouraged from following her plans. So they carried her away from them to a far-off land. The boy, meanwhile, fell into a deep sleep from the moment his beloved left home.

The family travelled for several years before returning to their old house. The girl was again sent to the brook one day, and there she saw the handsome young boy still asleep. She called his name, and he awoke. But he became an angel and started to fly away. No sooner had he left the ground, however, than he fell down and died immediately. Seeing that her lover had died, the girl also killed herself, and the two young people were buried together. They both became stars.

When they learned that their youngest brother had died so tragically, the five brothers also killed themselves, and all five of them became stars. They joined their young brother and the beautiful girl in heaven. Some day look for the seven stars and you will see them.

*The above story was taken from* 100 Armenian Tales and their Folkloristic Relevance, *collected and edited by Susie Hoogasian-Villa and published by Wayne State University Press, Detroit, 1966.*

**Bibliography**

Asbjørnsen, P.C. (ca. 1930) *Round the Yule Log: Norwegian Folk and Fairy Tales*, translated by H. L. Brækstad (modified by D.L. Ashliman), Philadelphia: J. B. Lippincott.

Ashliman, D.L. Folklore and Mythology Electronic Texts www.pitt.edu/~dash/folktexts.html (accessed 27/09/09).

Booker, C. (2004) *The Seven Basic Plots*, London: Continuum Books.

Fansler (1921) *Filipino Popular Tales*, Lancaster, Pennsylvania and New York: American Folk-Lore Society.

Hoogasian-Villa, S. (ed.) (1996) *100 Armenian Tales and their Folkloristic Relevance*, Detroit: Wayne State University Press.

Lyncker, K. (1854) *Deutsche Sagen und Sitten in hessischen Gauen,* Cassel: Verlag von Oswald Bertram.

Westcott, W.W. (1911) (3rd Edition) *Numbers, Their Occult Power and Mystic Virtues*, London, Benares: Theosophical Pub. Society. Scanned, proofed and formatted at sacred-texts.com, August 2009, by John Bruno Hare. This text is in the public domain in the US because it was published prior to 1923.

## Chapter 7
## WISDOM OF THE AGES

Though wisdom comes from experience as we learn from the mistakes we make along the way, frustratingly it often proves to be of little value. For, more often than not, what we have to offer is considered to be of no value by those who could most benefit from it. And, just like us before them, the only way our children will ever learn, despite all our efforts, is from their own mistakes too.

### The Pouch Full of Gold

One day a beggar happened to find a leather pouch that someone had dropped in the marketplace. Opening it, he discovered that it contained 100 pieces of gold. Then he heard a merchant shout, "A reward! A reward! There's a reward for the person who can find my leather pouch and return it to me!"

Being an honest man, the beggar came forward and handed the pouch over to the merchant saying, "Here's your pouch. May I have the reward now?"

"Reward?" scoffed the merchant, greedily counting his gold. "Why the pouch I dropped had two hundred pieces of gold in it. You've already stolen more than the reward! Go away or I'll call the police."

"I might be poor but I'm an honest man," said the beggar indignantly, "and you know very well I did no such thing. So let's us take this matter to the court."

In court, the judge patiently listened to both sides of the story and this is what he decided on:

"Citizens I believe you both. However, don't despair because justice is still possible! Merchant, you stated that the pouch you lost contained two hundred pieces of gold. Well, that's a considerable sum. But the pouch this beggar found only had one hundred pieces of gold in it, so it couldn't be the one you lost."

And, with that, the judge gave the pouch and all the gold to the poor but honest beggar who, if you ask me, more than deserved every last piece of it. What do you think?

**Growing Old**

I see you making exactly the same mistakes I made
When I was your age
And I try to stop you
But at the same time, I know,
Whatever I do or say
You're still certain you know best
Determined to do things your way
And there's absolutely nothing I can do to change things
The only thing I can really offer
Is to be here when you fall
And to avoid the temptation to say then
I told you so!

*As the following tale illustrates, growing older is not always about becoming wiser, for another (and somewhat unfortunate) characteristic of old age is developing a memory that can become rather selective:*

**How Mulla Nasruddin Sat in the Puddle**

Walking back home from his field after work one evening, Mulla Nasruddin found his pathway blocked by large a puddle. Feeling lazy, he couldn't be bothered to walk around it and so decided to jump across instead. He landed, however, right in the middle, and ended up completely soaked.

"How embarrassing! In my youth could have managed that easily", exclaimed the Mulla, looking all around. Having satisfied himself that nobody had been a witness to his shame, the Mulla then added, "To tell the truth, I was no better even in my youth!"

*"Armenia is perhaps the oldest of all the (predominantly) Christian countries in the world. It was a powerful nation at the advent of Christ, although at different periods in its history it was occupied by the Persians under Cyrus, the Macedonians under Alexander the Great, and the Romans under the Caesars*" (Kaeter, 2004, p.154). *In more recent times, to bring the story up to date, Armenia has been in the news due to the still unresolved conflict with Azerbaijan over the Nagorno-Karabakh region. The Armenian legend that follows about Solomon the Wise was adapted from Adolf Dirr's 1925 collection of tales, translated by Lucy Menzies:*

**Solomon the Wise and the Hermit**

During Solomon's reign, a hermit that people from far and wide made pilgrimages to visit, lived in a cave not far from Jerusalem. Solomon once made up his mind to go and visit him himself to ask for his advice, and took his favourite courtier with him. But the hermit knew through divine inspiration that the king was coming to him, and prepared for his reception by sweeping his cell and leaving the sweepings lying in the middle of it. Then he took off everything he was wearing, threw a cloth over his shoulders and waited on the threshold, holding his mouth with his right hand. When King Solomon and his courtier drew near, the latter said, "Sire, that's enough. Let's go home."

"Why then? If you remember, we came here for advice, so it would be a pity to go home without getting what we came for," Solomon replied.

"We have the advice already," the courtier said. "Come away and I'll explain it to you."

And when they got home the courtier gave the following explanation of what he had seen:

"The sweepings stand for our earthly possessions. By standing at his threshold, the hermit wanted to let us know that we are merely temporary inhabitants of this world. The cloth over his shoulders signified that all we need of the goods of this world is a winding-sheet. By holding his mouth he meant to tell us that man's most dangerous enemy is his tongue; he must keep it shut so that it may not babble."

The king was so well content with this explanation that he richly rewarded his courtier.

*The story that follows is about a king who was impatient to find the answer to this question, and what his impatience resulted in:*

**The King Who Would See Paradise**

Once upon a time there was king who, one day out hunting, came upon a fakir in a lonely place in the mountains. The fakir was seated on a little old bedstead reading the Koran, with his patched cloak thrown over his shoulders.

The king asked him what he was reading; and he said he was reading about Paradise, and praying that he might be worthy to enter there. Then they began to talk, and, by-and-bye, the king asked the fakir if he could show him a glimpse of Paradise, for he found it very difficult to believe in what he could not see. The fakir replied that he was asking a very difficult, and perhaps a very dangerous, thing; but that he would pray for him, and perhaps he might be able to do it; only he warned the king both against the dangers of his unbelief, and against the curiosity which prompted him to ask this thing. However, the king was not to be turned from his purpose, and he promised the fakir always to provide him with food, if he, in return, would pray for him. To this the fakir agreed, and so they parted.

Time went on, and the king always sent the old fakir his food according to his promise; but, whenever he sent to ask him when he was going to show him Paradise, the fakir always replied: 'Not yet, not yet!'

After a year or two had passed by, the king heard one day that the fakir was very ill— indeed, he was believed to be dying. Instantly he hurried off himself, and found that it was really true, and that the fakir was even then breathing his last. There and then the king besought him to remember his promise, and to show him a glimpse of Paradise. The dying fakir replied that if the king would come to his funeral, and, when the grave was filled in, and everyone else was gone away, he would come and lay his hand upon the grave, he would keep his word, and show him a glimpse of Paradise. At the same time he implored the king not to do this thing, but to be content to see Paradise when God called him there. Still the king's curiosity was so aroused that he would not give way.

Accordingly, after the fakir was dead, and had been buried, he stayed behind when all the rest went away; and then, when he was quite alone, he stepped forward, and laid his hand upon the grave! Instantly the ground opened, and the astonished king, peeping in, saw a flight of rough steps, and, at the bottom of them, the fakir sitting, just as he used to sit, on his rickety bedstead, reading the Koran!

At first the king was so surprised and frightened that he could only stare; but the fakir beckoned to him to come down, so, mustering up his courage, he boldly stepped down into the grave.

The fakir rose, and, making a sign to the king to follow, walked a few paces along a dark passage. Then he stopped, turned solemnly to his companion, and, with a movement of his hand, drew aside as it were a heavy curtain, and revealed—what? No one knows what was there shown to the king, nor did he ever tell anyone; but, when the fakir at length dropped the curtain, and the king turned to leave the place, he had had his glimpse of Paradise! Trembling in every limb, he staggered back along the passage, and stumbled up the steps out of the tomb into the fresh air again.

The dawn was breaking. It seemed odd to the king that he had been so long in the grave. It appeared but a few minutes ago that he had descended, passed along a few steps to the place where he had peeped beyond the veil, and returned again after perhaps five minutes of that wonderful view! And what WAS it he had seen? He racked his brains to remember, but he could not call to mind a single thing! How curious everything looked too! Why, his own city, which by now he was entering, seemed changed and strange to him! The sun was already up when he turned into the palace gate and entered the public durbar hall. It was full; and there upon the throne sat another king! The poor king, all bewildered, sat down and stared about him. Presently a chamberlain came across and asked him why he sat unbidden in the king's presence.

"But I am the king!" he cried.

"What king?" said the chamberlain.

"The true king of this country," said he indignantly.

Then the chamberlain went away, and spoke to the king who sat on the throne, and the old king heard words like 'mad,' 'age,' 'compassion.' Then the king on the throne called him to come forward, and, as he went, he caught sight of himself reflected in the polished steel shield of the bodyguard, and started back in horror! He was old, decrepit, dirty, and ragged! His long white beard and locks were unkempt, and straggled all over his chest and shoulders. Only one sign of royalty remained to him, and that was the signet ring upon his right hand. He dragged it off with shaking fingers and held it up to the king.

"Tell me who I am," he cried; "there is my signet, who once sat where you sit—even yesterday!"

The king looked at him compassionately, and examined the signet with curiosity. Then he commanded, and they brought out dusty records and archives of the kingdom, and old coins of previous reigns, and compared them faithfully. At last the king turned to the old man, and said:

"Old man, such a king as this whose signet thou hast, reigned seven hundred years ago; but he is said to have disappeared, none know whither; where got you the ring?"

Then the old man smote his breast, and cried out with a loud lamentation; for he understood that he, who was not content to wait patiently to see the Paradise of the faithful, had been judged already. And he turned and left the hall without a word, and went into the jungle, where he lived for twenty-five years a life of prayer and meditations, until at last the Angel of Death came to him, and mercifully released him, purged and purified through his punishment. [2]

2 This Pathan story, told to a Major Campbell, was taken from Lang, A (ed.) (1906) *The Orange Fairy Book,* London: Longmans, Green and Co. The book is copyright free and in the public domain.

*Edward Plunkett, the 18th Baron of Dunsany, (July 24, 1878-Oct 25, 1957) was known for his tales set in fantasy worlds, which were written under the pen name Lord Dunsany. He had a huge influence on H.P. Lovecraft, and his inventive fantasy paved the way for J.R.R. Tolkien. The following story can be found on the www.sacred-texts.com website. It comes from* The Book of Wonder *by Lord Dunsany (1912), and is in the public domain.*

**The Wonderful Window**

The old man in the Oriental-looking robe was being moved on by the police, and it was this that attracted to him and the parcel under his arm the attention of Mr. Sladden, whose livelihood was earned in the emporium of Messrs. Mergin and Chater, that is to say in their establishment.

Mr. Sladden had the reputation of being the silliest young man in Business; a touch of romance—a mere suggestion of it—would send his eyes gazing away as though the walls of the emporium were of gossamer and London itself a myth, instead of attending to customers.

Merely the fact that the dirty piece of paper that wrapped the old man's parcel was covered with Arabic writing was enough to give Mr. Sladden the ideas of romance, and he followed until the little crowd fell off and the stranger stopped by the kerb and unwrapped his parcel and prepared to sell the thing that was inside it. It was a little window in old wood with small panes set in lead; it was not much more than a foot in breadth and was under two feet long. Mr. Sladden had never before seen a window sold in the street, so he asked the price of it.

"Its price is all you possess," said the old man.

"Where did you get it?" said Mr. Sladden, for it was a strange window.

"I gave all that I possessed for it in the streets of Baghdad."

"Did you possess much?" said Mr. Sladden.

"I had all that I wanted," he said, "except this window."

"It must be a good window," said the young man.

"It is a magical window," said the old one.

"I have only ten shillings on me, but I have fifteen-and-six at home."

The old man thought for a while. "Then twenty-five-and-sixpence is the price of the window," he said.

It was only when the bargain was completed and the ten shillings paid and the strange old man was coming for his fifteen-and-six and to fit the magical window into his only room that it occurred to Mr. Sladden's mind that he did not want a window. And then they were at the door of the house in which he rented a room, and it seemed too late to explain.

The stranger demanded privacy when he fitted up the window, so Mr. Sladden remained outside the door at the top of a little flight of creaky stairs. He heard no sound of hammering.

And presently the strange old man came out with his faded yellow robe and his great beard, and his eyes on far-off places. "It is finished," he said, and he and the young man parted. And whether he remained a spot of colour and an anachronism in London, or whether he ever came again to Baghdad, and what dark hands kept on the circulation of his twenty-five-and-six, Mr. Sladden never knew.

Mr. Sladden entered the bare-boarded room in which he slept and spent all his indoor hours between closing-time and the hour at which Messrs. Mergin and Chater commenced. To the Penates of so dingy a room his neat frock-coat must have been a continual wonder. Mr. Sladden took it off and folded it carefully; and there was the old man's window rather high up in the wall. There had been no window in that wall hitherto, nor any ornament at all but a small cupboard, so when Mr. Sladden had put his frock-coat safely away he glanced through his new window. It was where his cupboard had been in which he kept his tea-things: they were all standing on the table now. When Mr. Sladden glanced through his new window it was late in a summer's evening; the butterflies some while ago would have closed their wings, though the bat would scarcely yet be drifting abroad—but this was in London: the shops were shut and street-lamps not yet lighted.

Mr. Sladden rubbed his eyes, then rubbed the window, and still he saw a sky of blazing blue, and far, far down beneath him, so that no sound came up from it or smoke of chimneys, a mediaeval city set with towers; brown roofs and cobbled streets, and then white walls and buttresses, and beyond them bright green fields and tiny streams. On the towers archers lolled, and along the walls were pikemen, and now and then a wagon went down some old-world street and lumbered through the gateway and out to the country, and now and then a wagon drew up to the city from the mist that was rolling with evening over the fields. Sometimes folks put their heads out of lattice windows, sometimes some idle troubadour seemed to sing, and nobody hurried or troubled about anything. Airy and dizzy though the distance was, for Mr. Sladden seemed higher above the city than any cathedral gargoyle, yet one clear detail he obtained as a clue: the banners floating from every tower over the idle archers had little golden dragons all over a pure white field.

He heard motor-buses roar by his other window, he heard the newsboys howling.

Mr. Sladden grew dreamier than ever after that on the premises, in the establishment of Messrs. Mergin and Chater. But in one matter he was wise and wakeful: he made continuous and careful inquiries about the golden dragons on a white flag, and talked to no one of his wonderful window. He came to know the flags of every king in Europe, he even dabbled in history, he made inquiries at shops that understood heraldry, but nowhere could he learn any trace of little dragons *or* on a field *argent*. And when it seemed that for him alone those golden dragons had fluttered he came to love them as an exile in some desert might love the lilies of his home or as a sick man might love swallows when he cannot easily live to another spring.

As soon as Messrs. Mergin and Chater closed, Mr. Sladden used to go back to his dingy room and gaze though the wonderful window until it grew dark in the city and the guard would go with a lantern round the ramparts and the night came up like velvet, full of strange stars. Another clue he tried to obtain one night by jotting down the shapes of the constellations, but this led him no further, for they were unlike any that shone upon either hemisphere.

Each day as soon as he woke he went first to the wonderful window, and there was the city, diminutive in the distance, all shining in the morning, and the golden dragons dancing in the sun, and the archers stretching themselves or swinging their arms on the tops of the windy towers. The window would not open, so that he never heard the songs that the troubadours sang down there beneath the gilded balconies; he did not even hear the belfries' chimes, though he saw the jackdaws routed every hour from their homes. And the first thing that he always did was to cast his eye round all the little towers that rose up from the ramparts to see that the little golden dragons were flying there on their flags. And when he saw them flaunting themselves on white folds from every tower against the marvelous deep blue of the sky he dressed contentedly, and, taking one last look, went off to his work with a glory in his mind. It would have been difficult for the customers of Messrs. Mergin and Chater to guess the precise ambition of Mr. Sladden as he walked before them in his neat frock-coat: it was that he might be a man-at-arms or an archer in order to fight for the little golden dragons that flew on a white flag for an unknown king in an inaccessible city. At first Mr. Sladden used to walk round and round the mean street that he lived in, but he gained no clue from that; and soon he noticed that quite different winds blew below his wonderful window from those that blew on the other side of the house.

In August the evenings began to grow shorter: this was the very remark that the other employees made to him at the emporium, so that he almost feared that they suspected his secret, and he had much less time for the wonderful window, for lights were few down there and they blinked out early.

One morning late in August, just before he went to Business, Mr. Sladden saw a company of pikemen running down the cobbled road towards the gateway of the mediaeval city—Golden Dragon City he used to call it alone in his own mind, but he never spoke of it to anyone. The next thing that he noticed was that the archers were handling round bundles of arrows in addition to the quivers which they wore. Heads were thrust out of windows more than usual, a woman ran out and called some children indoors, a knight rode down the street, and then more pikemen appeared along the walls, and all the jack-daws were in the air. In the street no troubadour sang. Mr. Sladden took one look along the towers to see that the flags were flying, and all the golden dragons were streaming in the wind. Then he had to go to Business. He took a bus back that evening and ran upstairs. Nothing seemed to be happening in Golden Dragon City except a crowd in the cobbled street that led down to the gateway; the archers seemed to be reclining as usual lazily in their towers, and then a white flag went down with all its golden dragons; he did not see at first that all the archers were dead. The crowd was pouring towards him, towards the precipitous wall from which he looked; men with a white flag covered with golden dragons were moving backwards slowly, men with another flag were pressing them, a flag on which there was one huge red bear. Another banner went down upon a tower. Then he saw it all: the golden dragons were being beaten—his little golden dragons. The men of the bear were coming under the window; what ever he threw from that height would fall with terrific force: fire-irons, coal, his clock, whatever he had—he would fight for his little golden dragons yet. A flame broke out from one of the towers and licked the feet of a reclining archer; he did not stir. And now the alien standard was out of sight directly underneath. Mr. Sladden broke the panes of the wonderful window and wrenched away with a poker the lead that held them. Just as the glass broke he saw a banner covered with golden dragons fluttering still, and then as he drew back to hurl the poker there came to him the scent of mysterious spices, and there was nothing there, not even the daylight, for behind the fragments of the wonderful window was nothing but that small cupboard in which he kept his tea-things.

And though Mr. Sladden is older now and knows more of the world, and even has a Business of his own, he has never been able to buy such another window, and has not ever since, either from books or men, heard any rumour at all of Golden Dragon City.

**Bibliography**

Dirr, A. (1925) *Caucasian Folk-tales*, London & Toronto: J.M. Dent & Sons Ltd.

Fatuyev, R. (1937) *The Pranks and Misadventures of the Mulla Nasr-Eddin*, Pyatigorsk: Ordzhonikidze Regional Publishing House (translated from the Russian by D.G.Hunt).

Kaeter, M. (2004) *The Caucasus Republics*, New York: Facts on File Inc.

## Chapter 8
## SHAMANIC COSMOLOGY TALES

Tribal cosmologies from throughout the world, however culturally distinct, seem to share the concept of a fundamentally three-tiered universe: the 'upper' world, associated with sky and space; the 'middle' world, associated with the surface of our earth and the human realm; and the 'lower' or 'under' world, associated with subterranean places and often described as the 'land of the dead' (Wilby, 2005, p.146).

What initially appear to be fairy tales for children often started out as something quite different. Take *Jack and the Beanstalk*, for example, which could well have started life as an account of a shamanic journey undertaken to the Upper World. The story presented below was probably at one time an account of a shamanic journey too, one undertaken to the Land of the Dead. It comes from a collection of Native American folklore, retold for children and young adults, over a century ago - *American Indian Fairy Tales* by Margaret Compton.

### The Island of Skeletons

Big Wave and his little nephew, Red Shell, lived together in a deep forest. The boy was the only relative that the old man had, and he was very fond of him. He had brought Red Shell and his sister, Wild Sage, to his home some years before, just after the great plague had killed most of his tribe, among them the father and mother of the children. But they had not been many months in the forest before Wild Sage was stolen by a giant who lived on the Island of Skeletons.

Big Wave warned the boy never to go towards the east; for, if by any chance, he should cross a certain magic line of sacred meal that Big Wave had drawn, he would be at the mercy of the giant.

The boy obeyed for a time; but by and by he grew tired of playing in one place, so he went towards the east, not noticing when he crossed the magic line, till he came to the shore of a great lake.

He amused himself for a while, throwing pebbles into the water, and shooting arrows. A man came up to him, and said, “Well, boy, where is your lodge?”

Red Shell told him. Then the man proposed shooting arrows to see who could shoot the higher. Red Shell had had much practice, and though he was only a boy, his arm was strong, and he drew the bow far back and sent the arrow much higher than the man did.

The man laughed and said, “You are a brave boy; now let us see whether you can swim as well as you can shoot.”

They jumped into the water and tried holding their breath while swimming. Again the boy proved himself the victor.

When they were again on land, the man said to him, “Will you go with me in my canoe? I am on my way to an island where there are pretty birds, and you can shoot as many as you please.”

Red Shell said he would go, and looked about for a canoe. The man began singing, and presently there appeared a canoe drawn by six white swans, three on either side. The boy and his companion stepped in and the man guided the swans by singing.

The island was so long that he could not see the end of it, but it was not very wide. It was thickly wooded and there was so much undergrowth that the ground could hardly be seen, but Red Shell noticed heaps of bones under the bushes, and asked what they were. He was told that the island had once been a famous hunting-ground and these were the bones of the animals that had been killed.

After wandering about for some time, the man proposed another swim. They had been in the water but a few minutes when the boy heard singing, and looking around he saw the man going off in the canoe and taking his own and Red Shell’s clothes with him. He shouted, but neither the man nor the birds paid any attention to him.

Thus he was left alone and naked, and it was fast growing dark. Then he remembered his uncle’s warnings, and was so miserable from cold, hunger and fear, that at last he sat down and cried.

By-and-by he heard a voice calling to him, “Hist! keep still.”

He looked round and saw a skeleton lying on the ground not far from him. It beckoned to him and said, “Poor boy, it was the same with me, but I will help you if you will do me a service. Go to that tree” (pointing to one close by) “dig on the west side of it, and you will find a pouch of smoking mixture and a pipe. Bring them to me. You can get a flint on the shore. Bring that also.”

The boy was terribly frightened, but the skeleton spoke kindly, and not as though he meant to do harm. Red Shell therefore went to the tree, and brought the pipe and smoking mixture. Then he found a flint and on being asked to do so struck fire, lit the pipe and handed the same to the skeleton.

It smoked quickly, drawing the smoke into the mouth and letting it escape between the ribs. Red Shell watched and saw mice run out from between the bones. When the skeleton was rid of them it said: "Now I feel better, and can tell you what to do to escape my fate. A giant is coming to-night with three dogs, to hunt you and kill you for his supper. You must lose the trail for them by jumping into the water many times on your way to a hollow tree, which you will find on the other side of the island. In the morning after they have gone, come to me."

Red Shell thanked the skeleton and started at once to find the tree. It was quite dark, so he could see nothing, but he ran from tree to tree, climbing hallway up each one, and running into the water many times before he found the place where he had been told to sleep.

Towards morning he heard the splash of a canoe in the water, and soon a giant followed by three large dogs, strode into the forest.

"You must hunt this animal," the giant said to the dogs.

They scented the trail and dashed through the bushes. They rushed up one tree and then another, and at last came back to the giant with their tails between their legs, for they had found nothing.

He was so angry that he struck the foremost animal with his war-club and killed it on the spot. He skinned it and ate it raw. Then he drove the two others down to the canoe, jumped in and went away.

When they were out of sight of the island, Red Shell crept from his hiding place and went back to the skeleton.

"You are still alive?" it asked in surprise. "You are a brave boy. To-night the man who brought you here will come to drink your blood. You must go down to the shore before the darkness comes and dig a pit in the sand. Lie down in it and cover yourself with sand. When he leaves his canoe, get into it and say 'Come swans, let us go home.' If the man calls you, you must not turn round or look at him. When you are free, do not forget the skeleton."

Red Shell promised to come back to the island and to do all that he could for the poor bones. He went down to the shore and dug the pit deep enough so that when he stood in it his head was on a level with the water. When he heard the song in the distance he knew the swans were coming; so he covered his head with sand and waited till he heard a footstep on the dry leaves.

Then he crept out stealthily, stepped into the canoe and whispered to the swans, "Come, let us go home." He began the song that he had heard their master sing to them, and the canoe glided from the shore.

The swans carried him down the lake to a large cleft rock in the center. They drew the canoe through the opening and through the cave till they came to a stone door. Red Shell tried to open it, but could not. Then he turned the canoe around and struck the door with the stern.

The door flew open and Red Shell found himself in a fine lodge. He saw his own clothes and many others heaped in a corner near the fire which was burning brightly. A kettle of soup was steaming over it and there were some potatoes in the ashes on the hearth.

Seeing no one, the boy ate supper and then lay down to sleep on a couch of wild-cat skins.

In the morning he went out and stepping into the canoe, said, "Come, swans, let us go to the island."

He saw the two dogs lying asleep in the sun and, on landing, found that then had killed their master.

The skeleton was delighted to see him and praised him for his courage and for being true to his word. But he said to him, "You must not go home yet. Travel toward the east three days and you will come to some huge rocks. There you will see a young girl drawing water from a spring. She is your sister, Wild Sage, whom the giant stole many moons since, and whom you believed dead. You will be able to get her away. When you have done so, come back to me."

Red Shell at once set out for the east and in three days he found the rocks of which he had been told. As he came near them he saw a lovely girl drawing water. "Sister," he said, going up to her, "you must come home with me."

She was frightened and tried to run away. Looking back, she saw that it was really her brother, when she was even more afraid, though she turned and spoke to him. "Hist," said she, "a giant keeps me here. Go before he sees you or he will kill you."

Red Shell did not move.

"Go," said Wild Sage.

"No," he answered, "not till you go with me. Take me to your lodge."

The giant had gone to a cranberry swamp, and Wild Sage knew that he would not return until the evening so she ventured to take her brother home with her. She dug a pit in one corner of the lodge, told him to get into it, and then covered it with her bed of buffalo skins.

Just before the darkness came the giant's dogs rushed in, barking furiously. "Who?" said the giant, "is hidden here?"

"No one," said Wild Sage.

"There is, there is," said the giant, "or the dogs would not bark like that."

They did not discover Red Shell, however, so the giant sat down to his supper.

"This boy is not tender, he is not cooked enough, get up and cook him more," said the giant.

"Cook it yourself, if it doesn't suit you," she answered.

The giant took no notice of her answer, but called to her to come and take off his moccasins.

"Take them off yourself," she said.

"Kaw," thought the giant, "now I know she has some one hidden. I will kill him in the morning."

Early the next day the giant said he was going to the cranberry swamp to get some children for his dinner. He did not go far from the lodge, but hid himself in some bushes close to the shore.

He saw Wild Sage and her brother get into a canoe, and threw a hook after them, which caught the boat and drew it towards the shore. But Red Shell took up a stone and broke the hook, and they floated off once more.

The giant was in a terrible rage. He lay down flat on the ground, and, putting his mouth to the water, drank so fast that the canoe was drawn close to the shore He began to swell from drinking such a quantity, and could not move. Red Shell took another stone and threw it at him. It struck him and he snapped in two, and the water he had swallowed flowed back into the lake.

Red Shell and his sister then sailed to the island, where the two dogs who had eaten their master rushed down to meet them. The boy raised his hand threateningly, and said: "Off to the woods as wolves. You no longer deserve to be dogs."

The animals slunk away growling, and as they disappeared were seen to change into lean and hungry wolves.

Red Shell went to the skeleton, who commanded him to gather all the bones that he could find on the island and to lay them side by side in one place. Then he was to say to them, "Dead folk, arise!"

It took him and his sister many days, for there were bones everywhere. When all had been arranged in one place, Red Shell stood off at a little distance and called loudly, “Dead folk, arise!” The bones raised themselves and took human form. All the men had bows and arrows, but some had only one arm, and others only one leg. The skeleton whom Red Shell had first met became a tall, handsome warrior, perfect in every limb. He saluted Red Shell as Chief, and the others did the same.

Then the boy and his sister crossed the lake and travelled westward till they came to their uncles’ lodge. He was very old, his fire was out and he was still mourning for his nephew. But as he listened to the story of the lad’s adventures, and realized that he had come back unhurt, some of his years left him.

They built a long lodge with many fireplaces; then Red Shell returned to the island and brought back those who had been skeletons. The handsome brave, who was known as White Eagle, married Wild Sage, and they all dwelt together in peace to the end of their lives.

By rescuing Wild Sage from the Island of Skeletons, Red Shell plays the role of a psychopomp in this tale, a role that the shaman would have played - as the one who leads the dead person to his or her final resting place or, in this case, back from it to this world again. And the magic line the boy is warned not to cross at the start of the story, marks the barrier between the two worlds.

The word psychopomp, etymologically, means “a deliverer of souls” and is derived from two Ancient Greek words, *psyche* meaning ‘soul’ or ‘spirit’ and *pompos* meaning ‘sending’. Other examples of figures who have acted as psychopomps include Ganesh the doorkeeper in Hindu mythology, Hermes, Mercury, the Greek Ferryman of the River Styx, the Christian Holy Spirit, the Egyptian Anubis, and the Norse Heimdal. The Greeks and Romans believed the dead were ferried across the river Styx by a boatman named Charon, and they paid him by placing a coin in the mouth of the deceased.

The Nisqually, a Salish tribe, are located on the Nisqually River in rural Thurston County, 15 miles east of Olympia, Washington. The name Nisqually has also been extended to apply to those tribes on the east side of Puget Sound who speak the same dialect, including the Puyallup, Skagit,

Snohomish, Snokwalmu and Stilakwamish. We know from the 1857 field notes of the first territorial survey of the region that it was the practice of some of the Indian tribal groups to use the very small islands of southern Puget Sound as burial islands and Ka-ka-als, a little island of less than twenty acres, is known to be one of those places. An alternative name for Ka-ka-als is 'Grave Island, no doubt because of the multitude of Indian graves the early settlers found there. The island was the obvious place for a cemetery as not only was it close to home but it also provided safety from wild animals (see Carpenter, 1996, p.18). Cemeteries are located on islands in other cultures too. Among the Senoi Temiars of Malaysia, for example, "Graves are always situated across water, usually the other side of a river, as the dead person's ghost is thought to have difficulty in traversing water" (Jennings, 1995, p.93), and the ghost is thus deterred from returning to the village to haunt people. Consequently, the fact that the skeletons are to be found on an island would have come as no surprise to those for whom the tale was originally intended.

As for the canoe drawn by six white swans that features in the tale, Spirit Canoes or water craft are one of the chief hallmarks of shamans throughout the circumpolar area, from Scandinavia and Siberia to Greenland. In the old days, when the lone shaman's power was not considered to be sufficient to affect a cure, the Spirit Canoe ceremony would be performed to help the person who needed healing.

They are not ordinary canoes, but magical vessels (charged with sacred and cosmological significance) that can penetrate the earth, fly across space, or ascend up to the sky … In shamanistic ideology the boat is often a vehicle of the gods, of spirits, or of shamans on their journeys to other worlds. In Siberia, for example, the Ostyak shaman sets out in such a symbolic voyage to the other world in order to retrieve his patient's soul. Among the Coast Salish on the west coast of North America, the most elaborate instance of this shamanistic conception is ritualized and given artistic expression. (Vastokas and Vastokas, 1973, pp.128 & 126, cited in Miller, 1988, p.97.)

*To conclude this chapter, there follows the both moving and memorable account of an American Indian* Journey to the Land of the Dead. *Before the spirit of the departed starts his Journey to the nether world, he is carefully informed of the surprises and dangers of the voyage and is duly instructed how to overcome them.*

**The Winnebago Indian Road to the Land of the Dead**

I suppose you are not far away, that indeed you are right behind me. Here is the tobacco and here is the pipe which you must keep in front of you as you go along. Here also are the fire and the food which your relatives have prepared for your journey.

In the morning when the sun rises you are to start. You will not have gone very far before you come to a wide road. That is the road you must take. As you go along you will notice something on your road. Take your war club and strike it and throw it behind you. Then go on without looking back. As you go farther you will again come across some obstacle. Strike it and throw it behind you and do not look back. Farther on you will come across some animals, and these also you must strike and throw behind you. Then go on and do not look back. The objects you throw behind you will come to those relatives whom you have left behind you on earth. They will represent victory in war, riches, and animals for food.

When you have gone but a short distance from the last place where you threw the objects behind, you will come to a round lodge and there you will find an old woman. She is the one who is to give you further information. She will ask you, "Grandson, what is your name?" This you must tell her. Then you must say,

"Grandmother, when I was about to start from the earth I was given the following objects with which I was to act as mediator between you and the human beings (i.e., the pipe, tobacco, and food)." Then you must put the stem of the pipe in the old woman's mouth and say,

"Grandmother, I have made all my relatives lonesome, my parents, my brothers, and all the others. I would therefore like to have them obtain victory in war, and honours. That was my desire as I left them downhearted upon the earth. I would that they could have all that life which I left behind me on earth. This is what they asked. This, likewise, they asked me, that they should not have to travel on this road for some time to come. They also asked to be blessed with those things that people are accustomed to have on earth. All this they wanted me to ask of you when I started from, the earth. They told me to follow the four steps that would be imprinted with blue marks, grandmother."

"Well, grandson, you are young but you are wise. It is good. I will now boil some food for you." Thus she will speak to you and then put a kettle on the fire and boil some rice for you. If you eat it you will have a headache. Then she will say,

"Grandson, you have a headache, let me cup it for you." Then she will break open your skull and take out your brains and you will forget all about your people on earth and where you came from. You will not worry about your relatives. You will become like a holy spirit. Your thoughts will not go as far as the earth, as there will be nothing carnal about you.

Now the rice that the old woman will boil will really be lice. For that reason you will be finished with everything evil. Then you will go on stepping in the four footsteps mentioned before and that were imprinted with blue earth. You are to take the four steps because the road will fork there. All your relatives who died before you will be there. As you journey on you will come to a fire running across the earth from one end to the other. There will be a bridge across it but it will be difficult to cross because it is continually swinging. However, you will be le to cross it safely, for you have all the guides about whom the warriors spoke to you. They will take you over and take care of you.

Well, we have told you a good road to take. If anyone tells a falsehood in speaking of the spirit-road, you will fall off the bridge and be burned. However you need not worry for you will pass over safely. As you proceed from that place the spirits will come to meet you and take you to the village where the chief lives. There you will give him the tobacco and ask for those objects of which we spoke to you, the same you asked of the old woman There you will meet all the relatives that died before you. They will be living in a large lodge. This you must enter. (Paul Radin, "The Winnebago Tribe", in Thirty-eighth Annual Report, Bureau of American Ethnology, Washington, D.C., 1923, pp. 143-4).

*What can be seen from this is that the select few can transform the shamanic journey "into one with marked affiliations to the memorable journey of Dante, with its proper division into a* via purgativa*, a* via illuminative*, and a* via unitiva *and then to transfer it to this world" (Radin, 1957, p.166) so that the divine experience can become a preparation for the earthly experience, rather than the reverse. In other words, what is learnt in non-ordinary reality can be* *transferred to and applied in this reality and, in the same way, what can be learnt through a story can be transferred to and applied to this reality.*

**Bibliography**

Carpenter, C.S. (1996) *Tears of Internment: The Indian History of Fox Island and the Puget Sound Indian War*, Tacoma, Washington: Tahoma Research Service.

Compton, M. (1907) *American Indian Fairy Tales*, New York: Dodd, Mead & Company. Scanned at sacred-texts.com, February 2007. This text is in the public domain in the United States because it was published prior to January 1st, 1923. These files may be used for any non-commercial purpose provided this notice of attribution is left intact in all copies.

Jennings, S. (1995) *Theatre, Ritual and Transformation: The Senoi Temiars*, London: Routledge.

Miller, J. (1988) *Shamanic Odyssey: The Lushootseed Salish Journey to the Land of the Dead*, Menlo Park, California: Ballena Press.

Radin, P. (1923) *The Winnebago Tribe*, in Thirty-eighth Annual Report, Bureau of American Ethnology, Washington, D.C.

—. (1957 2nd Edition) *Primitive Man as Philosopher*, NewYork: Dover (originally published in 1927).

—. (1957) *Primitive Religion*, Dover Publications Inc. (first published in 1937 by the Viking Press).

Vastokas, J. and Vastokas, R. (1973) *Sacred Art of the Algonkians: A Study of the Peterborough Petroglyphs*, Peterborough: Mansard Press.

Wilby, E. (2005) *Cunning Folk and Familiar Spirits: Shamanistic Viisionary Traditions in Early Modern British Witchcraft and Magic*, Eastbourne: Sussex Academic Press.

## Chapter 9
## INTO THE DREAMTIME

The riches that we long for and travel far and wide in search of, can often be found where we least expect them to be - on our own doorstep - as the man in the following tale finds out. It has been adapted from a story in *The Book of the Thousand Nights and a Night,* translated by Richard F. Burton (London: The Burton Club, 1885) Since its first translation into a European language between 1704 and 1717, *The Thousand and One Nights,* also known as *The Arabian Nights,* has been recognized as a universal classic of fantasy narrative. It is, in fact, a much older work. Based on Indian, Persian, and Arab folklore, it dates back at least 1000 years as a unified collection, with many of its individual stories undoubtedly being even older. If this particular story seems familiar to you, it might be because it provided the basis for the modern classic - Paolo Coelho's *The Alchemist*:

**The Man Who Became Rich through a Dream**

Once there lived in Baghdad a wealthy businessman who lost all his means and was then forced to earn his living by hard labour. One night a man came to him in a dream, saying,

"Your fortune is in Cairo; go there and seek it." So he set out for Cairo. He arrived there after dark and took shelter for the night in a mosque. As Allah would have it, a band of thieves entered the mosque in order to break into an adjoining house. The noise awakened the owners, who called for help. The Chief of Police and his men came to their aid. The robbers escaped, but when the police entered the mosque they found the man from Baghdad asleep there. They laid hold of him and beat him with palm rods until he was nearly dead, then threw him into jail.

Three days later the Chief of Police sent for him and asked, "Where do you come from?"

"From Baghdad," he answered.

"And what brought you to Cairo?"

"A man came to me in a dream and told me to come to Cairo to find my fortune," answered the man from Baghdad, "But when I came here, the promised fortune proved to be the palm rods you so generously gave to me."

"You fool," said the Chief of Police, laughing until his wisdom teeth showed. "A man has come to me three times in a dream and has described a house in Baghdad where a great sum of money is supposedly buried beneath a fountain in the garden. He told me to go there and take it, but I stayed here. You, however, have foolishly journeyed from place to place, putting all your faith in a dream which was nothing more than a meaningless hallucination." He then gave him some money saying, "This will help you return to your own country."

The man took the money. He realized that the Chief of Police had just described his own house in Baghdad, so he returned home immediately, where he discovered a great treasure beneath the fountain in his garden. And this is how Allah brought the dream's prediction to fulfilment.

*The same tale can be found in many different traditions and there follows a Yiddish version:*

**The Treasure at Home**

One night, Isaac, the son of Rabbi Yekl, dreamed that there was a chest of treasure hidden under the Praga side of the Warsaw bridge. So he travelled to Warsaw. At the bridge he tried to reach the spot, but a soldier was standing guard there. So he paced up and down as he waited for the soldier to go away. The soldier meanwhile became aware of someone on the bridge, so he went up to Isaac and asked him what he wanted. Isaac told him the truth: that he had dreamed about a chest of treasure buried under the bridge. The soldier said,

"I've never heard of anything so ridiculous. Just because I dreamed about a treasure in the oven at the home of Isaac, Rabbi Yekl's son in Cracow, doesn't mean I have to go there!"

Isaac turned around and went home, where he took his oven apart and found a chest of treasure that made him a very rich man.

*Some people seem to do little else than dream. In fact, they seem to dream their whole lives away, like the man in the following Indian folktale. It has been adapted from a story in* Folklore of the Santal Parganas *by Cecil Henry Bompas (London: David Nutt, 1909)*

**The Daydreamer**

Once a man who sold oil was going to market with his pots of oil arranged on a flat basket, and he engaged a Santal for two *annas* to carry the basket. And as he went along, the Santal thought:

With one *anna* I will buy food and with the other I will buy chickens, and the chickens will grow up and multiply, and then I will sell some of the fowls and eggs, and with the money I will buy goats. And when the goats increase, I will sell some and buy cows, and then I will exchange some of the calves for she-buffaloes, and when the buffaloes breed, I will sell some and buy land and start cultivation, and then I will marry and have children, and I will hurry back from my work in the fields, and my wife will bring me water, and I will have a rest, and my children will say to me, "Father, be quick and wash your hands for dinner," but I will shake my head and say, "No, no, not yet!"

And as he thought about it he really shook his head, and the basket fell to the ground, and all the pots of oil were smashed.

Not surprisingly, the oil man was furious and told the Santal that he must pay two rupees for the oil and one anna for the pots. But the Santal said that he had lost much more than that, and the oil man asked him how that could be. The Santal explained how with his wages he was going to get fowls and then goats and then oxen and buffaloes and land, and how he came to spill the basket, and at that the man who sold oil roared with laughter and said,

"Well, I've added everything up and I find that our losses are equal, so we can call it quits." And so saying they went their ways laughing.

*The almost supernatural power of artists to bring pictures to life is the subject of the next story, based on a traditional Japanese fairytale. Most doodling can probably be described as innocuous. However, the drawings of cats produced by the boy in this story are clearly a great deal more than that. Perhaps if we believe in something strongly enough and, more importantly, in our own power, we can then dance our dreams awake.*

**The Boy Who Drew Cats**

A long time ago, in a little Japanese village, there lived a poor farmer with his wife and four children. The oldest son was strong and healthy and helped the farmer in the fields every day and the two daughters worked with their mother in the house. But the youngest son, although he was extremely clever, was also quite small and frail. He could not work in the rice fields with his father and brother.

One day the boy's parents began to discuss his future, since he was not suited to being a farmer. His mother said, "Our younger son is very clever. Perhaps we should apprentice him to the local priest. The priest is getting old and it may be that our son will make a good priest and a suitable helper for the old one." The boy's father agreed with his wife and they went to the village temple to ask the priest to accept their son.

The priest interviewed the boy and was impressed by his ability and the imaginative answers he gave to his questions. So the old priest agreed to take the boy as long as he promised to obey him. The boy tried very hard to obey and he learned many things, but unfortunately he had one failing. When he should have been studying his lessons on his own, the boy drew cats instead. He could not help himself, for he was an artist at heart. He drew big cats and small cats, fat cats and thin cats, tall cats and short cats, sweet cats and ferocious cats. He drew cats in his notebooks, he drew cats on the floor, he drew cats on the walls and, worst of all, he drew cats on the big, white, rice paper screens in the temple itself.

The old priest was angry at first, and told the boy that drawing cats when he should be studying was wrong. But then the priest became sadder and sadder, because the boy continued to draw cats when he should have been working on his lessons. Soon the priest told the boy that he had no choice but to ask him to leave and return to his home. The priest said his good-byes and gave the boy one piece of advice. He said, "Avoid large places at night, keep to small." Then the priest went into his room and closed the door. The boy did not understand what the priest meant, but he was afraid to knock on the door to ask for an explanation. He packed his few belongings into a bundle and went on his way.

When the little boy reached the road, he thought, "If I go home, my parents will be angry and will punish me. Maybe I should go to the big city and see if the priests in the temple there could use a new apprentice." So he turned away from his home and headed for the city. No one had told the boy that the grand temple in the city had been closed. The boy took his time and enjoyed the walk to the city, looking at the fields and birds and butterflies.

It was dark when the boy arrived at the city gates, and everyone was in bed asleep. There was no one to tell him that an evil goblin had taken over the temple and chased all the priests away. There was no one to tell him that many soldiers had tried to rid the temple of the goblin rat, but had failed. Boldly, he walked up to the temple door and knocked on it. Because there was no answer, he knocked several more times. When there still was no answer, he turned the handle and pushed on the door. It swung wide open, and the boy walked in calling, "Is anyone here?" No one answered him, but he thought that a priest would come by eventually. The boy saw that there was a little room near the door, so he went in and sat down to wait.

Now the goblin always left a light burning in the temple in order to lure strangers in at night. But the little boy knew nothing about this, so he just waited. While he was looking around, he opened the drawer in a table and found some rice paper, pens and ink. Soon he was filling the paper with drawings of cats. When he ran out of paper, he drew cats on the floor. And then he just couldn't help himself. He had to draw cats on the white, paper screens in the temple. He drew and drew until they were covered with cats.

When he had filled the screens with pictures of every kind of cat he could imagine, the little boy was very tired. He started to lie down next to one of the screens. But just then the words of the old priest ran through his mind, "Avoid large places, keep to small." The temple was enormous, so the boy looked around for a small place. He found a tiny cupboard in the little room near the door and climbed into it with his parcel of clothes. He shut the cabinet door and was soon fast asleep on a shelf, with his bundle for a pillow. In the middle of the night, the boy heard a loud sound of fighting. It sounded like howling and running and thumping and bumping and growling. He peeked out of his hiding place, but it was too dark to see anything and he was so frightened that he just closed the cabinet door and stayed inside.

In the morning the boy opened the cupboard and crawled out. He tiptoed out of the little room and peeked into the temple. What a surprise! The immense, evil goblin was dead, lying on the temple floor. Who could have killed him? Then the little boy looked at the temple screens. Each cat that he had drawn had a little circle of red around its mouth. Then the boy knew that his cats had attacked and killed the goblin. And he now understood what the priest meant when he said, "Avoid large places, keep to small."

When the people of the city discovered that the goblin had been defeated, they proclaimed the boy a hero. The priests of that temple would have been happy to take him in, but the little boy had changed his mind. He did not want to become a priest. He became an artist instead, a very successful one, and his paintings of cats became famous all over the land.

*To ensure an attentive audience while telling a story, you can interrupt the narrative to interpolate the word shoes; and unless the learners immediately respond socks, break off the tale without finishing it! This is a distinctive storytelling convention used in certain Gypsy communities. A dream of a delicious meal lands on the plate of a Gypsy in the following tale as a result of his ingenuity:*

**The Dream**

Once there was a Gypsy hammering away at a pot behind a hedge, where he was taking shelter from the wind. A rabbit passed by, and the Gypsy threw his hammer at it. Exactly at that moment a hunter shot at the rabbit. The rabbit fell dead, and the two quarrelled over whose it was.

"Okay," said the Gypsy. "If you invite me for dinner to your house, we can think about what to do."

They went home, and the hunter's wife prepared a fine dinner for them. Finally the Gypsy said, "Listen, I know what we'll do. At this point the rabbit is neither yours nor mine. We'll go to sleep, and the rabbit will belong to whoever has the more beautiful dream. And don't worry about me: just give me an old blanket and I can sleep on the floor here in the kitchen near the stove."

And that's what they did. The hunter went upstairs with his wife, and the Gypsy stretched out on the kitchen floor.

Morning came. The hunter came downstairs and said, "Okay, let's get started. Tell me your dream."

"No, no, tell me yours first. You're more important than I am."

"Then I'll tell mine. Last night in my dream I saw a magnificent spiral staircase. I kept climbing up and up … At a certain moment the heavens opened and I entered paradise: flowers, light, music. I couldn't possibly tell you how beautiful it was. Well it was so beautiful that I didn't want to return. And you, what was your dream?"

"Oddly enough, I had the same dream. I saw you climbing that spiral staircase into heaven. And I naturally assumed you wouldn't want to come back, so I ate the rabbit."

*Our dreams, both waking and sleeping, can provide us with valuable lessons, as proves to be the case for the head of the clan in the following Chinese tale:*

**Dreams**

The head of the Yin clan in the state of Chou had an enormous estate, and his servants worked without rest from dawn until dusk. There was one aged servant whose muscles were sapped of all strength, but the head of the clan only drove him all the harder. The old man groaned as he faced his tasks each day, and at night he slept like a log, totally exhausted from all the work he had done. And each night he dreamed that he was king of the realm, presiding over all the people, taking full command of the affairs of state. He feasted carefree in the palace, and every wish was gratified. His pleasure was boundless. But every morning he awoke and went back to work again.

To those who tried to comfort him for the harshness of his lot, the old man would say, "Man lives a hundred years, half in days, half in nights. By day I'm a common servant, and the pains of my life are as they are. But by night I'm lord over men, and there can surely be no greater satisfaction. So what have I got to resent?"

The mind of the clan head was occupied with worldly affairs; his attention was taken up with his estate. Worn out in mind and body, he too was totally exhausted by the time he went to bed. But night after night he dreamed he was a servant, rushing about trying to complete all his tasks. For this he was rebuked and scolded or beaten with a stick, and he took whatever he got without complaint. He mumbled and moaned in his sleep and quietened down only when dawn approached.

The head of the clan took his problem to a friend, who said, "Your position gives you far more wealth and honour than other men have. Your dream that you're a servant is nothing more than the cycle of comfort and hardship; this has always been the norm of human fortune. How could you expect to have both your dream and your waking life the same?"

The head of the clan reflected on his friend's opinion and decided to ease the workload of his servants as a result. This way he also reduced his own worries, finally giving himself some relief from his dreams.

*Is this the reality or is this the dream? Sometimes we just cannot seem to see which is which and work out what really matters in life, and that is what this tale is all about:*

**The Confirmation**

I had been going there on a regular basis for twenty years, accompanying my mother, but nothing like it had ever happened before. We said the usual prayers, shed the usual tears, the sun came out of the clouds as it always did on these occasions, and we felt better for the emotional release as we always did - but something, I felt, was still missing. I wanted us all to be close together again, just as it used to be, and just as I knew we all would be again one day. So I put my hand on the stone that bore the inscription. And when I did so the following words came to me, nothing more and nothing less, from a faraway place, a place free of worries and cares - *"Enjoy life more!"*

How easy it was for him, to hit the nail on the head, and make me focus on the one thing I have long forgotten how to do. Perhaps somehow he knows my days are short and does not want me to end my life with regrets about all the things I never got round to. Like he did, wanting me to live my life to the fill, right up to the very last minute. Wish I could. But, knowing me, I would just make it into a task to accomplish and end up getting no pleasure out of it in any case.

Anyhow, the fact that my good intention to follow the advice was unlikely to last, even until the end of the day, was in a way irrelevant. What was important, what mattered, was the confirmation.

Then it was back into the everyday world again, the long drive home along the motorway, the stop in an impersonal service station for an overpriced and tasteless cup of tea, the background music over the loudspeakers, and everything forgotten - until the next time. So much time spent sleeping, with just the occasional flashes of insight that whiz by before you even get the chance to notice. And life goes on, just as it always has done, just as it always does, and just as it always will do.

## Chapter 10
## A WINDOW ON THE CAUCASUS

Spending any length of time in a region as ethnically diverse and conflict-ridden as the Caucasus means constantly having to walk a conversational tightrope. Everything from ordering a coffee (it may be called *Turkuli* - Turkish coffee - in Georgia, but in Yerevan you'd better say Armenian coffee) to place names (Karabakh's ancient city is Shushi to Armenians, Shusha to Azerbaijanis) is a potential minefield for the unwary traveller.

Learning to be diplomatic - often by just keeping your mouth shut - is the key to navigating Caucasus conversations. But it's not always easy. Armenians, Azerbaijanis and Georgians (not to mention Abkhaz, Ossetians, and the dozens of other peoples scattered around the region) are passionate about their histories and love a good argument.

One especially contentious topic is the subject of 'firsts'. As home to some of the world's oldest civilisations, the Caucasus is rife with arguments about who did what first - who were the first people to adopt Christianity, who were the first to invent a written alphabet, and who were the first to settle a particular patch of land. And the competition to claim firsts can lead to a lot of good-natured teasing.

There is a popular joke in Armenia, for example, about how Mesrop Mashtots, the inventor of the Armenian alphabet, had also invented the Georgian alphabet by throwing a leftover plate of spaghetti on the floor. The Georgians also have a joke they never tire of telling visitors to their country that makes fun of how Armenians always claim to have done everything first. It's about a team of Georgian archaeologists claiming to have discovered wires in an ancient site, proving that Georgians were the first to have telephone lines. The next day, so the joke goes, the Armenians discovered a site without wires and claimed to have had mobile phones instead. At other times, the debate over 'firsts' can be deadly serious, like when discussing the territorial struggles - over Abkhazia, Nagorny Karabakh or South Ossetia.

What can be generally agreed on, though, is that the Caucasus is undoubtedly one of the cradles of civilization - the land with which the earliest folklore of Europe is connected, the land where Noah's Ark is said to have settled, and the land of the Argonauts and of Prometheus. It is also a region that has been called the geopolitical pivot about which everything sways - American economic interests, Russian American economic interests, Russian territorial interests, and Islamic religious interests. It is a place where mountains reach the sky, where continents meet, where empires used to intersect and where a multitude of languages mix. Additionally, it can be described as a place where unimaginable, unspoiled beauty and everyday barbarity can be found side by side.

The story that follows is about the legendary hospitality of the people, and it comes from the Republic of Georgia:

**An Old Guest**

At the beginning of the harvest each year people used to celebrate the event. One day everyone is out, dressed up and working in the fields, but doing nothing too arduous because it is a time for celebration. Among those people there are three poor brothers who have no food and only a little a*raq'i* (*chacha*) to drink. Everyone is sitting down for dinner. They are feasting and singing.

Suddenly an old man came and said *gamarjoba* (hello) to everyone but nobody invited him to the table. When he passed by the three brothers, though, the youngest brother said "Let's invite him".

The brothers said "What can we offer him to eat or drink?"

"We can offer him what we have."

He didn't ask again and called the man, "Could you please honour us and come for a short time?"

The guest said, "Everyone is feasting and singing, so why aren't you?"

"What can we do? We have no food, and only very little drink. How can we feast?"

The guest said to the youngest brother, "Not to worry, pour what you do have and let's drink together." The youngest brother poured the drinks. And it's a wonderful wine!

"You don't have bread, do you?" asked the guest, and then "Can you see something white on that mountain? What is that then? Go and bring it here!"

"That's a stone. Why should I bring it here?"

"You go and bring it and then we'll see!"

The youngest brother went to the mountain. He saw a beautiful big sheep and white bread. Now the brothers can really lay the table. They sat down and started singing. They were singing so well that others stopped what they were doing to listen to them. Who are those singing this way!

The workers are laughing: what on earth could they have, that they have even been able to invite a quest! Those beggars are so poor that it's hard to imagine what they could give him to eat or drink.

When they finished eating the old man asked the oldest brother, "What would you prefer to have? What do you like most of all?"

"I would like land to grow food on!"

"You'll have land and food, as much as you could possibly ever want, for as long as you don't get tired of having guests and entertaining them," and then he blessed the land.

Now the old guest asked the middle brother "What would you prefer to have? What do you like most of all?"

"I'd like cattle," said the middle brother

"Nobody will have as many cattle as you. You'll have as many as you could possibly ever want, for as long as you don't get tired of having guests and entertaining them."

And finally he asked the same question to the youngest brother, "What would you like most of all?"

"I'd like to have a wife who would love guests and hosts, who would look after the family," said the youngest brother.

"Oh dear, I only know two women like that in this world, one is already married and the other is getting married today. I'll try to change things, though, so she marries you instead."

Two bothers settled down there. One brother had land and bread, the second one had cattle, and the old man took the youngest brother with him.

A son of one king was marrying a daughter of another king. It was their wedding day. The old man bought wind and rain with him and he went to the place where the reception was being held and said to the people who were assembled there, "We don't have anywhere to stay tonight. Can we stay with you?"

The king was told but he refused to allow it, "If I let strangers attend the wedding celebrations, it might cause problems. I won't let anyone in tonight and after that I'll decide if I'll let you in or not."

The old man kicked the door open and went in regardless, taking the youngest brother with him. The table was laid. The bride and bridegroom were sitting together. The old man and the boy were sitting opposite the newly-weds. The old man said to the boy:

"Go get the bridegroom from his seat and you sit down there."

The boy did as he was told. The king was furious, "That's why I didn't want to let you in."

The old man said, "Don't talk nonsense! The bride belongs to him, not the bridegroom."

The king got more furious, "Let's bet on whether he is the rightful husband or not."

"What bet can there be? We don't need to bet because that woman is already married," said the king. But then he changed his mind and asked, "What kind of bet were you thinking of?"

"Let's give each of these men a branch of a vine, and see in whose hands the branch grows leaves, blossoms, and then produces grapes which ripen, and that we would then be able to eat at the table. And we'll give the wife to that person."

The king didn't want to agree but there was no way of going back by then and he knew it. So he gave both men a branch of a vine. In the hands of the younger brother the branch sprouted leaves, blossomed, produced grapes, and the grapes ripened. But the branch of the king's son remained as dry as a bone.

"Will you give the girl to the younger brother now?" asked the old man.

"No, I won't. She is already married."

"Then let the man who can dance on this sword be the one."

The king's son was the first to get up and dance, but each time he stepped on the blade of the sword he cut his feet.

"Now it is your turn, to get up and dance," the old man told the youngest brother. The boy got up and danced on the sword without any problem.

"Now we can take the woman," the old man said to the king

"No, you're not taking her, and that's final!"

But the guests got up and left, and the woman got up too and left with them. Nobody could stop her. The old man helped them to settle down, blessed them and said,

"Nobody can ever be happier than the two of you unless there comes a point when you hate having guests."

Time passed and all the brothers lived happily. One day the same old man was passing by - he was St George. It was raining; it was horrible out, such bad weather that nobody would wish to be out in it. The old man stood in front of the oldest brother's door.

"Show some charity! Let me stay with you. It's raining heavily outside."

"My wife burnt her hand by baking the bread for the last guests we had and, because of that, this time I won't let anyone in," said the oldest brother.

"Whatever fortune you had before, you will have the same again," said the old man.

Then he stood in front of the middle brother's door and said, "Show some charity! Let me stay with you. It's raining heavily outside."

"My wife burnt her hand by baking the bread for the last guests we had and, because of that, this time I won't let anyone in," the middle brother answered the same way the oldest had.

"Whatever fortune you had before, you will have the same again," said the old man.

At last the old man stood in front of the youngest brother's door. Only his wife was at home. Her husband had just died and she was at the side of his coffin, crying.

"Hostess, hostess, good woman, let me stay with you tonight." The grieving woman looked out:

"Do come in, please, and I will sweep the floor in a minute." The woman wiped the tears from her eyes, hid the coffin in a dark corner, tidied the house, started the fire, killed a hen and invited the guest in.

"Oh, I didn't know that you were alone. Where's your husband?" the old man asked.

"Yes, I am on my own at the moment. My husband went to the market, and he hasn't come back yet," said the heartbroken woman.

The guest knew that her husband was dead and he was in the coffin in the dark corner of the room. The guest got up pretending that he wanted to go out. He went to the dark corner, lifted up the lid of the coffin, blew over him, and the youngest brother came back to life again. And this time he was even better looking than he had been before. The old man held him by the hand and they went into the room together.

"Why were you so late?" asked the woman, trying not to show the guest her true feelings.

"I already know everything. You're a very good woman and you will have a great fortune," said the old man. He blessed the youngest brother and his wife, said goodbye, and left.

Ever since that time, the youngest brother has become richer and happier but his brothers poorer and poorer, and anything but happy with their lot in life.

*The number of people who, when they hear the name 'Georgia,' think immediately of a state in the USA is decreasing fast. And those who know that Georgia is a small but vibrant country in the Caucasus, with a fantastic climate, and an unequalled reputation for hospitality and wine-growing are fast becoming the majority.*

*Georgian belongs to the Kartvelian group of Iberian-Caucasian languages, and is one of the oldest of the living languages. The Assyrian manuscript "A book of peoples and countries", written in the fifth century, contains a note that of 73 peoples then known only 14 had a written language. Among these Georgians are mentioned (Latin, Slavic-Cyrillic, Arabian, Indian, Chines, Japanese, Korean, Ethiopian, Greek, Georgian, Armenian, Jewish, Mongolian and Syrian). As for the Georgian alphabet, it has the same number of letters as there are sounds, so spelling and pronunciation are identical. Handwriting and printing are similar too, making Georgian orthography one of the simplest and most perfect in the world. The Georgian written language was created under King Parnavaz (III century AD).*

*It is said that God first came upon the Georgians only after he had already allocated all the countries of the world to the various nationalities. The Georgians, being in typically festive mood, invited the Creator to join them in wine and song. And the Lord so enjoyed himself that he decided to give these merry and carefree people the one spot on the earth that he had reserved for himself - the sunny valleys and hills that lie to the south of the Great Caucasus Mountains. The Lord has lavished great bounties on this land. It is a land of contrasts, of savage mountains snow-topped and swept with wild gales, of tumultuous rivers and dark forests; and of vast, warm plains and pasturage and valleys soft with tropical heat. Its mountains are stored with minerals and its valleys are smiling with corn and flowers.*

*Due to its special position between Europe and Asia - at the crossroads of peoples, cultures and languages - since early times Georgia has been a place of passage and enormous migrations. Peace has been permanently sought by the peoples in this part of world, but without much success, and the life of Georgians has been a constant and tragic fight for the preservation of their land and liberty.*

*In view of the fact that the people are predominantly Orthodox Christian, the message we find in the tale that follows, that we cannot necessarily look forward to justice in the next world, would at first seem to be somewhat surprising. On the other hand, given the constant struggle that has been their lot, a certain degree of bitterness and cynicism is only to be expected.*

**The Poor Servant and the Rich Nobleman**

There was a poor boy who became the servant of a rich nobleman. This nobleman treated him really badly though, by making him work both day and night, leaving him to starve most days, and by beating him pitilessly. One day the poor boy said,

"My nobleman's treating me very badly in this world but, no matter, because he'll be judged in the other world for his deeds."

The poor boy passed away in less than a year's time after he had started to work for the nobleman. When the boy died, that same day the nobleman got ill from eating too much. He did everything he could to cling on to life, primarily because he had so much wealth and he did not want to lose it. But death would not let him escape from what fate had in store for him, and so he died too.

The boy was on his way to the other world and the nobleman caught him up with him. The boy said,

"Aha! Now he'll be judged for what he did to me!"

They both approached a place where they found two guards who had clearly been expecting them,

"We've been waiting so long for you! Where have you been all this time?" they asked the boy. One guard hit the boy from one side and another one from the other side. The boy said to himself,

"I was hit hard so many times, but let's wait and see how many times they hit him!"

Next, the nobleman approached the guards, dressed in an expensive fur coat and a hat, and the guards treated him with the greatest of respect. The boy thought,

"This means nothing; we'll be judged when and where it's time for our proper judgment."

They then came to the place where the judgment of the other world normally takes place. Six men were sitting around a table, and there was a pillar with a rope hanging from it - a rope with a noose at the end, a rope for someone to be hanged from. And there were a pair of scales too, scales to weigh the sins committed by a man against the good deeds done by him. The boy was told:

"Stop and tell us about the sins you've committed and the good deeds you've done then." The boy said,

"I don't have any sins to confess to. I'm a sinless but worn out man." After that he was asked,

"Did you used to go to church?"

"No, not me. Who would allow me to go to church? I was working all day and night."

"Did you ever light candles?"

"No, I never had money for them."

"Then you must be a very sinful person with all sorts of wrong doings to confess to, and you deserve to go to hell. At least you could have kissed a priest on his hand. Didn't you at least do that?"

"No, I never did."

"So you deserve an even greater hell. Have you ever worked on Sundays?"

"What do you think? Do you think my nobleman would ever give me a rest? Look - here he is too, right next to me, the man responsible for all my suffering!" But the guards paid no attention to what he told them.

"Take this boy and throw him into the greatest hell." The guard was about to take him away, but the boy asked:

"Here is my nobleman. Please, before you take me away, let me stay for his judgment." The guard stopped. The nobleman approached the judges next.

"You need to tell us about your sins and good deeds now," the judges said. The nobleman replied,

"I've done nothing wrong in my life. I'm as sinless as a sheep."

"Did you ever go to church?"

"Of course I did. Every weekend I was there."

"Good, good. And did you light candles?"

"The candles I used to light were so enormous that, and I tell no lie, they were as big as I am!"

"Then you deserve paradise. And did you kiss the priests' hands?"

"Of course. I used to invite them to parties and made a lot of donations to the church too."

"It's clear from all you've told us that you're a sinless man," the judges praised him. "Have you ever worked on Sundays, though?"

"What do you think? I didn't even work on any other day of the week so why would I have been working on Sundays?" Then the judges told the guards,

"Take him to paradise, open the doors of paradise wide for him, and seat him on a golden chair."

The boy was flabbergasted by their verdict, and shouted to the people of this world,

"Poor people, like me, there is no justice at all here (in the other world). The truth is that paradise and hell are both to be found on earth, and anyone who thinks otherwise is unfortunately just deluding himself."

# Chapter 11
# HOW THE FLOWERS CAME TO BE

Flowers have played important roles in society from ancient times to the present. The rose, for example, has been cultivated in China for over 5000 years. In ancient Greece and throughout the Roman Empire flowers were used as symbols of human feeling and passion, and there are numerous biblical references to flowers. Throughout time, each culture has ascribed its own meanings to individual flowers. For example in Victorian England, the carnation was given to someone as a wish for good luck, but in Korea it was used to tell a young woman's fortune. She would place three in her hair. If the top died first, she was doomed to unhappy days in her old age. If the middle died first, she would have a woeful youth. If the bottom flower died first, her whole life would be a disaster. In Japan, the chrysanthemum is regarded as a symbol of long life in happiness; in fact, their Emperor sat upon the Chrysanthemum Throne in a significant demonstration of this belief. As for their neighbours in ancient China, nobility there so valued the chrysanthemum heraldry may be found. The French royal coat of arms in the 12th century showed the image of the flower of the lily (fleur-de-lys). Later, the English adopted the rose and placed it on the badges under their coats of arms; in Scotland they chose the thistle, in Wales the leek, and in Ireland it was the shamrock.

During the $19^{th}$ century in Europe, the idea of having a national flower became important in the search for a symbol of unity. For example, Germany chose as its flower the knapweed (*Centaurea*) and the Slovenians chose the carnation. Other European countries chose different flowers, depending on their position in popular culture. The tulip is for everyone a synonymous with Holland, the corn poppy with Poland, and thyme with Bohemia. In Eastern Europe the camomile flower is preferred in Russia, in Belarus the flax and in Ukraine the sunflower. Some countries use flowers to represent particular ideologies, as for example the use of the tied wheat sheaf to represent socialism. It is evident that the images of flowers play an integral role in the ethnic and political definition of the world, as well as helping us to understand and appreciate each other more fully.

In Victorian England the meaning of flowers was raised to an art form. Not only did each flower have its own meaning, but the way it was presented was equally important. For instance, an inverted flower took on the exact opposite of its meaning were it presented bloom-side up. Combinations of flowers were used to express various shades of sentiment and meaning, subtle or otherwise. A pair of roses, one red and one white, presented together implied unity between the giver and the receiver. If the white one was withered, however, it implied that first impressions were transient. Flowers were also used to pass coded messages between people, most often between lovers who had to conceal their emotions from watchful chaperones. The colour, combination of flowers, and the way they were presented all took on special significance within this coded language. Taking flowers by the right hand could mean "yes," while taking them with the left hand would mean "no."

However, more important than valuing flowers for how we can use them to transmit messages, is perhaps something else much more fundamental. And all the stories included in this section of the book, despite the fact that they come from many different cultures and sources, have one thing in common - they help to renew our sense of wonderment at the daily miracles that take place all around us and help to prevent us from taking what we have been blessed with for granted.

Hyacinths are one of the most beautiful and long lasting spring flowers, often producing a heavy but pleasing scent depending on the variety. Hyacinthus was an attractive Spartan youth much in favour with the Greek Gods Apollo and Zephyrus. According to Greek mythology, Apollo accidentally killed Hyacinthus while teaching him to throw the discus. An alternative version of the story is that Zephyrus was jealous of the attention Apollo gave to Hyacinthus and caused the discus to strike Hyacinthus and kill him. The tale that follows comes from Romania:

**The Story of the Hyacinth**

The hyacinth was once a girl named Hyacinth and fate had not been too kind to her, because both her parents had died when she was still a child and she had no other relatives on Earth. So she grew up very lonely and became an extremely hardworking girl, in fact the most diligent girl in the village. Besides that, she was also as good as gold and grew more and more beautiful by the day. All the girls in the village envied her and so none of the families wanted to give her work to do any longer. Therefore life became harder and harder for Hyacinth and she was desperately unhappy.

But one day God read the big *Book of Life* and he saw how miserable Hyacinth was and also the unhappiness that was going to befall her in the future. Among her troubles her husband was going to be a lazy, good-for-nothing drunkard. Saint Peter and the Holy Virgin took pity on Hyacinth and asked God if he could help her. So God decided to change the girl's destiny and make her happy. He summoned the two wanderers of the time, Prier and Florar. Prier, young and playful, was the one who kept the Earth dry. Florar, a little older than Prier, had violet eyes and his hair was of the green grass, full of flowers. He would make the Earth green and wake up the flowers in spring, just by gently blowing over them. God turned both of them into young men and sent them down to Earth, so that one of them could marry Hyacinth.

Meeting Hyacinth, the two men greeted her and she answered "Thanks to one of you". Curious as to which of them she had thanked, they asked her and she replied that she had thanked the one who would guess the answer to a riddle. Florar guessed the answer correctly and so he married her. But because he was not a real man, but a servant of God and lived in Heaven, he could not take Hyacinth with him so he turned her into a flower. Ever since that day, wandering through the world every spring and summer, Florar spreads Hyacinth's seed all over it.

*Whatever efforts we make to protect the people or possessions we value, the truth is we can never be sure of anything in this life, as Sakaki learns to his cost in the following tale. That is why it is so important to make the most of what we have, every minute of every day, because we can never know how long we will have it for.*

**The Bamboo Princess**

Once upon a time there was an old man whose name was Sakaki and he made baskets from bamboo shoots. One day he went to the bamboo grove as usual and he found a shiny golden shoot growing there. When he cut it open, there was a beautiful baby inside. As you can imagine, nothing like this had ever happened to him before and he was very surprised. He carried the baby carefully back to his house to show his wife.

"What a beautiful baby she is!" his wife exclaimed. They decided to call her Kaguya Hime - the Bamboo Princess.

When Sakaki returned to the bamboo grove the following day, he found other golden bamboo shoots growing there and they were filled with gold coins so he suddenly became a very rich man.

Kaguya Hime grew up to be the most beautiful woman in the whole of Japan and her reputation spread far and wide. Three great men heard of her beauty and offered to marry her. But she didn't want to get married to anybody so she gave them a task to perform that she knew would be impossible.

"I'll marry you if you can take a crystal ball from the hand of a dragon and bring it to me." And the Bamboo Princess gave them just three weeks to accomplish the task.

The first man did indeed manage to return with a crystal ball but when the princess saw it she shook her head. "I'll never marry you because you cheated. I can see you paid a glass cutter to make the crystal for you." As for the second man, he didn't bring back anything with him. "The task you set us was impossible because the dragon's crystal ball only exists in fairy stories," he said angrily. The third man was unable to return with anything either. And this is what he had to say: "I went to the end of the world in search of the crystal and tried as hard as I could but I have to admit the task was beyond me." The he lifted up his shirt to reveal a dreadful scar on his chest, which was the proof of the hardships he had been through. So the Bamboo Princess didn't have to marry anyone and was safe for the moment.

However, a few weeks later Sakaki received a letter from the King saying he wanted to marry the princess. Sakaki was of course overjoyed when he heard the news but Kaguya Hime was certainly not. It was the last thing on earth that she wanted to do.

There was a full moon in the sky that night and the Bamboo Princess just sat staring at it and couldn't stop crying.

"My dearest bamboo princess, why are you so sad?" Sakaki asked gently.

"Father the time has come for me to tell you the truth," she replied. "I'm not who I seem to be. I'm not of this world and I come from the moon where I now have to return to. And they will come for me on the night of the next full moon so I only have one more month with you."

"Oh my princess, how can this be? I couldn't bear to be parted from you. Nobody will take you away from me and I promise that somehow I'll manage to protect you and keep you here." Sakaki said fiercely.

The next morning, true to his word, he started to build a high wall around the house, hired security guards to patrol the area and asked the King to provide help too. The King came personally to the house with a thousand of his bravest soldiers and they were all armed with bows and arrows. But the Bamboo Princess was still crying because she knew all their efforts were pointless.

"Mummy and daddy, thank you so much for everything you've done for me and you can be sure I'll never forget you as long as I live. But look, they're already coming for me," and she pointed up to the sky above.

The King commanded his soldiers to draw their bows and prepare for battle. But the next moment a dazzling light filled the sky and temporarily blinded them all. Once it had passed and they were able to open their eyes again, the Bamboo Princess had gone and was never seen again.

The Bamboo Princess *is reputed to be one of the oldest Japanese folk tales and was first recorded in the ninth century.*

Of all the kinds of good practices,
Filial piety is the first.
Of all the myriad evils,
Licentiousness is the worst.

*The Chinese say true filial conduct can move the heavens and Meng-Chung, in the traditional tale that follows, was undoubtedly a paragon of filial virtue:*

**Winter Bamboo Shoots**

On a chilly winter day, Meng-Chung's mother, who had a serious illness and was on her deathbed, told Meng-Chung that all she wanted to do was to be able to have one final meal of her favourite food - delicious bamboo shoots. Meng-Chung was so devoted to her that he would do anything he possibly could to please her. He knew, however, that at that time there was no bamboo trees that produced shoots in winter. Meng-Chung went to the forest and searched high and low to find his mother's favourite food. However, despite all his efforts, he could not find any bamboo shoots at all. Knowing how ill his mother was and how he had been unable to provide her with the one thing she longed for, Meng-Chung started to cry. His tears touched the hearts of the gods in heaven and one of them used his mighty power to allow the bamboo plants to produce their shoots immediately. Meng-Chung was delighted. He collected as many shoots as he could carry and then cooked them to feed his mother. She was so delighted to be able to eat her favourite food in winter that she started to recover from her illness. From that time on, the bamboo plant started to produce shoots in winter on a regular basis. To commemorate Chung's devotion to his mother, the Chinese people started to call the shoots Mengchung bamboo shoots and the tree Mengchung bamboo.

*The botanical name of the winter bamboo is* Phyllostachys pubescens mazel *or* Phyllostachy edulis. *In China and in Taiwan people call this kind of bamboo* Mengchung Chu. Chu *means bamboo and the name comes from an ancient Chinese story. There are twenty four most honourable sons in ancient Chinese history and Meng-Chung is one of them.*

**The Origin of Xian-Fei Bamboo**

More than 4,000 years ago, when Yao was Emperor and growing old, he decided to abdicate in favour of a younger man. After taking some time to consider all the candidates, he came to the conclusion that Yu-Shun, a thirty year-old farmer who was well respected for his virtuous behaviour and loyalty to his parents, would be the right man for the job. So Yao arranged for his two beautiful daughters, Erh-Huang and Nu-Ying, to marry Yu-Shun. Yu-Shun became the new Emperor, devoting himself to caring for his people and managing his lands, and he enjoyed a happy and fulfilling family life with his two wives. But when Yu-Shun grew older, the Yellow River flooded. The land was covered with water everywhere and looked like an ocean. Houses were underwater, loads of horses and cattle were carried away by the flood, and the people had no food or shelter. Realizing how serious the problem was, the Emperor turned to Da Yu to deal with the situation, and Da Yu spent nine years completing the job.

At that time, there were nine notorious dragons that had killed many people and destroyed whole villages in Chang-Wu, which was the ancient name for China's Kuang-Hsi province. Despite his age and frailty, Yu-Shun decided to lead an army to Chang-Wu to kill the dragons, and to reward Da Yu for his success in dealing with the flood by making him the new Emperor. Erh-Huang and Nu-Ying feared for their husband's safety. They waited and waited and waited but had little news of their husband. Day after day, month after month, they stood by the door looking down the road to see if he was on his way home to them. Several years passed by but still Yu-Shun failed to return. Eventually the two queens could not bear the situation any longer and they set out in search of their husband. When they arrived in Xian-Chiang (chiang means river, Xian is he ancient name for China's Hu-Nana province), a river which flowed towards Tung-Ting lake (China's biggest lake), they heard the news they had been dreading - the news of Yu-Shun's death in Chung-Wu.

They started to cry and their tears fell on the bamboo shoots that grew by the lake. It is said that all of the "tears" on the bamboo show how much the two queens cried on hearing the news of Yu-Shun's death. Finally they threw themselves into the river to follow their husband into the next world. Nowadays people can visit their tombs near the place where they committed suicide. Both of them were named Xian-Fei (fei means queen in Chinese) after that. And the spotted bamboo by the lake was named Xian-Fei bamboo in memory of the two loyal wives of Yu-Shun.

*There is an old Sussex legend that St. Leonard fought against a great dragon in the woods near Horsham, only defeating it after a mortal combat lasting many hours, during which he received grievous wounds, but wherever his blood fell, Lilies-of-the-Valley sprang up to commemorate the desperate fight, and these woods, which bear the name of St. Leonard's Forest to this day, are still thickly carpeted with them. It is said that the fragrance of the Lily-of-the-*

*Valley draws the nightingale from hedge and bush, and leads him to choose his mate in the recesses of the glade.*

**The Lily of the Valley**

Once upon a time there lived in a village a beautiful girl named Margarita (Coral) and she loved a young man called Voinea (The Brave). The villagers called him Voinea because he was the most courageous of all the young men in that part of the world. He loved Margarita and they used to meet every evening after sunset at a cliff called by the old ones the Cliff of Flowers.

The Tartars used to plunder the country at that time and the Khan fell in love with Margarita. He was afraid of Voinea and swore to kill him and steal the girl. So, one day he hid behind a rock and shot seven poisonous arrows at Voinea. They hit him in seven places, blood spurted out of the wounds, and Voinea fell to his knees. Margarita covered him with kisses and bitter tears started to fall from her eyes, but there was nothing she could do to save him and Voinea bled to death.

Heartbroken and driven half crazy with grief, Margarita strangled the Khan with her belt and pushed him over the cliff. The old men say that the girl went mad because of what happened and for a long time after this tragic event, a shadow would wander about the cliff weeping and wailing. They also say that the blood from Voinea's wounds turned the flowers it fell on red and they became known as 'Voines's Blood'. The flowers Margarita's tears fell on turned white in colour and they were called 'margaritel' (corals). The cliff is known as the Tartar's Cliff and the rock Voinea fell from became known as the Rock of the Death.

*Ancient legends tell us the lily sprang from the milk of Hera, the mythological Queen of Heaven, and it is considered by artists and poets to be the only flower with a soul. According to old English folklore, lilies spontaneously grew on the graves of innocent people who had been wrongly executed.*

*The lily is also mentioned in the Bible. Often called the "white-robed apostles of hope" lilies were found growing in the Garden of Gethsemane after Christ's crucifixion. White lilies are said to have sprung up where drops of Christ's sweat fell to the ground from the cross. Traditionally, Easter Lilies are arranged in churches, during Easter, to commemorate the resurrection of Jesus Christ.*

**The Legend of the Lily**

Once upon a time there was a palace in the middle of a forest that had formerly belonged to Zmeul Zmeilor (The Greatest Dragon). But it was now inhabited by a wicked witch. During the day she had a human face but at night she would turn into a bird or a snake and terrorize people. Anyone who dared to approach the palace would be turned into a flower and she held thousands of innocent souls captive this way.

During that time, two children were sent away from home and while they were wandering through the forest, hungry and tired, they happened to come across the palace. The girl drew near and she was suddenly turned into a flower. The witch then picked the flower and took it back to her palace.

The boy continued to wander through the world, lonely and sad. He prayed to God to help him find his sister, but he got tired and decided to work for a shepherd. He often went to the forest but he was always careful not to get to close to the palace in case what had happened to his sister happened to him too. At night, he used to play his pipe with his eyes full of tears. One night he fell asleep in the forest. He dreamt that he was wandering through dark places and had found a beautiful flower, picked it up and took it to the palace. When he touched something with that flower, the spell cast by the wicked witch was broken. When he got up in the morning he started to look for the flower and after a few days he eventually found it. He cried and laughed with happiness because it meant he could now find his beloved sister.

When he arrived at the palace, the wicked witch was fortunately nowhere to be seen. The boy found the flower his sister had been turned into, touched it with his special flower, and it turned back into a girl again. The boy and his sister were overjoyed to be reunited. Not surprisingly, they both wanted to leave the palace as quickly as possible, but the gate could not be opened. It had been made to shut forever. The poor boy shook and rattled the gate but there was nothing he could do.

Upon hearing the noise, the witch came to see what was going on and, when she saw the children, turned them both into flowers. However, she died in the process because she had used up all her magical powers. The palace became a ruin and grass began to grow on its walls. Two big white sweetly scented flowers grew near the gate of the palace and these were the two children who had been turned into lilies.

**The Rose**

Greek mythology has an unusual tale to explain the origin of the rose. Rondanthe was a beautiful Greek maiden. So beautiful, in fact, that she was constantly followed by hopeful suitors, spellbound by her beauty. Rodanthe, however, had no interest in any of them and ignored them completely. The goddess Diana was enraged by the stupid behaviour of the young men, exasperated by the dismissive attitude of Rodanthe, and jealous that she herself was not the object of this attention. In her anger, Diana turned Rodanthe into a rose and the suitors into the rose's thorns.

The Romans told a different story. Mourning the death of her beloved Adonis, Venus wept in a garden. As her tears fell they turned into beautiful white roses. Her son Cupid was in the garden at the time, practising with his bow and arrows. Suddenly he was stung by a bee. His shots went awry and stuck into the stems of roses, becoming the thorns. When Venus tore her foot on a thorn drops of blood fell and became red roses.

Prized for centuries for their beauty and as a source of perfume, roses are probably the world's most widely cultivated ornamental plants. Many traditions tell of the first rose. The Arabs believed the first rose to have sprung from a drop of sweat from the brow of Mohamed. In Christian tradition, the original Rose grew in the Garden of Eden and it had no thorns. The thorns were only added after man's fall.

As a heaven sent flower, the Rose is the most frequently mentioned flower in legend of the saints. One of these tells the story of how a maiden, unjustly accused of wrong doing, was condemned to be burned to death. As the flames were about to be lit, she called to God to deliver her and make her innocence clear to all men. As soon as the flames leapt around her, they were suddenly extinguished, the wood turning into freshly sprouting rose bushes. Those pieces not yet alight showing pure white blooms, those already kindled glowing with crimson blooms. Ever since then the rose has been the emblem of Christian martyrdom.

**The Singing Rose**

A king had three beautiful young daughters. He thought about making one of his daughters queen, but he did not know which one to choose. One day he summoned all three and said to them,

"My dear children, I'm old and frail now, and every day is a gift. But before I die, I'd like to attend to all my unfinished business and name one of you as the heir to my kingdom. Now go out into the big wide world, and the one of you who brings back a singing rose shall inherit my throne and become the new queen."

When the three daughters heard this, they tearfully took leave of their old father, then - trusting their luck - set out for foreign lands, each taking a different path.

It happened that the youngest and most beautiful of them had to go through a dark pine forest. All kinds of birds were singing at the same time and it was wonderful to listen to them. When it began to get dark, the birds flew to their nests, and after a while it became as quiet as a mouse. Then suddenly a heavenly sound could be heard, such as the princess had never heard before, neither from birds nor from humans, and she immediately thought,

"That can only be the singing rose." She hurried on in the direction that the exquisite sounds seemed to be coming from. She had not walked long before she saw a large, old-fashioned castle on a cliff. She eagerly climbed up to the castle and pulled several times on the latch. Finally the gate opened with a creaking sound, and an old man with a long, ice-grey beard looked out.

"What do you want?" he grumpily asked the startled maiden.

"I'm looking for a singing rose," she answered. "Do you by any chance happen to have such a thing in your garden?"

"Yes indeed," answered the old man.

"What do you want for it?"

"You need give me nothing for the singing rose and you can have it today. But as payment, I will come for you in seven years and bring you back with me to this, my castle."

"Whatever you say. Just bring it to me," shouted the maiden joyfully, for she was thinking only about the singing rose and the kingdom, not about what would happen in seven years time.

The old man went back into the castle and then returned with it. The rose was singing so beautifully that the maiden's heart jumped for joy. She eagerly reached out her hand for the flower, and as soon as she had it in her hands she headed off home.

The old man called after her with a serious voice,

"Remember. In seven years time then!" But the maiden was not listening and her thoughts were already on other things.

She wandered the entire night through the dark woods with her rose, and her pleasure caused her to forget any fear she may have had. As for the rose, it sang continuously and the louder and more beautifully it sang, the faster the princess hurried on home.

The first thing she did when arrived was to tell her father everything that had happened and to present the rose to him. The rose sang beautifully, the king was overjoyed, and the castle was witness to one celebration after the other. As for the two older sisters, they had found nothing, and had had to return home empty handed. And now the youngest daughter, who had brought back the rose, became queen, although the old father continued to rule, and they all lived happily together. Day after day and year after year slipped by.

Finally the seventh year came to an end, and on the first day of the eighth year the old man from the castle appeared before the king and demanded his payment. The king presented to him his oldest daughter, but the old man was not fooled and rejected her. When the king saw that he could not get away with deception, he was left with no choice but to turn over the youngest and dearest of his children to the old man.

The princess now had to go with the grumbling greybeard to his castle, from which she had once obtained the singing rose. The beautiful maiden was very sad, for she had no one there except for her old master. In the castle there were plenty of other pleasures, but they did not comfort her, for she did not have the company of her loved ones. Her thoughts were always in her homeland. To make matters even worse, all the doors and chests in the castle were locked, and the old man did not let her have access to a single key.

One day she learned that her oldest sister was to marry a neighbouring prince, and that the wedding would take place in a few days. Disquieted, she went to the old man and asked him for permission to attend.

"Go then!" growled the old man, "But I'm telling you in advance, make sure you don't laugh even once when you're there. If you disobey my order, I'll tear you into a thousand pieces. I myself will continually be by your side, and if you as much as open your mouth to laugh, it will be over with you. Be warned!"

The princess thought that this would be easy to follow, and on the announced day she appeared at the wedding with the old greybeard at her side. Joy ruled in the king's castle when they saw the long missing queen returning. She was very happy and took advantage of the day, but she did not forget the old man's order, and she did not once open her mouth to laugh. That evening she had to take leave from her loved ones, and she sadly returned to the lonely castle with her companion. Her boring life continued just as it had done before.

Then she heard the news that her other sister was about to get married too. This disquieted her again, and she asked the old man if she could not attend her second sister's wedding.

"Go then!" growled the old man." But this time you're not allowed to speak a single word the entire day. And I'll go with you again to make sure of it.

The princess thought that this would be easy to follow, and on the announced day she appeared with the old greybeard at her side. Joy ruled in the king's castle when they saw the long missing queen returning, and everyone ran out to meet her and to hear all her news.

But she pretended that she could not talk, and did not allow a single sound to escape from her beautiful lips. But this time she did not keep up her courage as well as she had the last time, and that evening when everyone was talking together, a little word inadvertently slipped out. The old man quickly jumped up, took her by the hand, and led her out of the hall and back to his lonely castle.

Like before, she greatly missed the company of her loved ones, and everything seemed terribly monotonous to her. But one day when she was sadly walking through the garden where the rose had previously blossomed and sung, the old man came to her and said with a serious expression,

"Your majesty, if tomorrow while it is striking twelve you cut off my head in three blows, then everything that you find in the castle will be yours, and you'll be free forever!" The princess took heart from the old man's speech and decided to attempt the risky deed.

The next day - it was Saturday - the old man appeared a little before twelve o'clock and uncovered his neck. She drew the sword that she had hung about her waist, and as the castle clock struck for the first time she swung the sword once, then quickly again two more times. The old man's head rolled away on the floor. But instead of blood, a key fell from it - the key that opened all the chests and doors in the castle. There the princess found many, many precious things, and she was rich and free forever. [3]

---

3 This Austrian folktale has been adapted from a story in *Kinder- und Hausmärchen* by Ignaz and Joseph Zingerle (Innsbruck: Verlag der Wagner'schen Buchhandlung, 1852)

**Echo and Narcissus**

Echo was a beautiful nymph, fond of the woods and hills, where she liked to play. She was one of Diana's favourites and accompanied her when she went hunting. But Echo had one failing; she was much too fond of talking, and always insisted on having the last word.

One day Juno was looking for her husband, who, she had reason to believe, was amusing himself among the nymphs. Echo by her talk managed to detain the goddess until the nymphs had made their escape. When Juno discovered what Echo had done, this is what she decided upon: "You shall forfeit the use of that tongue with which you have cheated me, except for that one purpose you are so fond of - reply. You shall still have the last word, but no power to speak first."

One day Echo noticed Narcissus, a handsome youth, while he was out hunting in the mountains. She was fascinated by him and followed his footsteps. How she longed to speak to him and to win him over! But it was no longer in her power. She waited with impatience for him to speak first, and had her answer ready. One day the youth, being separated from his companions, shouted aloud,

"Who's here?" Echo replied,

"Here." Narcissus looked around, but seeing no one called out,

"Come." Echo answered,

"Come." As no one came, Narcissus called again,

"Why do you shun me?" Echo asked the same question.

"Let's join each other," said the youth. The maid answered with all her heart in the same words, and hastened to the spot, ready to throw her arms around him. He started back, exclaiming,

"Hands off! I would rather die than you should have me!"

"Have me," she said; but it was all in vain. He left her, and she went to hide her blushes in the recesses of the woods. From that time onwards she lived in caves and spent her days roaming the mountain sides. Her form faded with grief, till at last all her flesh shrank away. Her bones were changed into rocks and there was nothing left of her but her voice. Even after all this time, however, she is still ready to reply to anyone who calls her, and still keeps up her old habit of always insisting on having the last word.

Narcissus's cruelty in this case was not the only instance. He shunned all the rest of the nymphs, just as he had shunned poor Echo. One day a maiden who had in vain endeavoured to attract him uttered a prayer that he might some time or other feel what it was to love someone and to receive no affection in return. The avenging goddess heard and granted the prayer.

There was a clear fountain, with water like silver, to which the shepherds never drove their flocks, nor the mountain goats resorted, nor any of the beasts of the forest; neither was it defaced with fallen leaves or branches; but the grass grew fresh around it, and the rocks sheltered it from the sun.

One day Narcissus came upon it - hot, tired and thirsty. He stooped down to drink, and saw his own image in the water; he thought it was some beautiful water-spirit living in the fountain. He stood gazing with admiration at those bright eyes, the curly locks, the rounded cheeks, the ivory neck, the parted lips, and the healthy glow. He fell in love with himself. He brought his lips near to take a kiss; he plunged his arms in to embrace the beloved object. It fled at the touch, but returned again after a moment and renewed the fascination. He could not tear himself away; he lost all thought of food or rest, while he hovered over the brink of the fountain gazing upon his own image. He talked with the supposed spirit:

"Why, beautiful being, do you shun me? Surely my face is not one to repel you. The nymphs love me, and you yourself are clearly not indifferent to me. When I stretch out my arms you do the same, you smile upon me, and respond to my gestures too." His tears fell into the water and disturbed the image. As he saw it depart, he exclaimed,

"Stay, I entreat you! Let me at least gaze upon you, if I may not touch you." With this, and much more of the same kind, he cherished the flame that consumed him, so that by degrees he lost his colour, his vigour, and the beauty which formerly had so charmed the nymph Echo. She kept near him, however, and when he exclaimed,

"Alas! Alas!" she answered him with the same words.

He pined away and died; and when his shade passed the Stygian river, it leaned over the boat to catch a look of itself in the waters. The nymphs mourned for him, especially the water-nymphs; and when they beat their breasts Echo beat hers also. They prepared a funeral pile and would have burned the body, but it was nowhere to be found. In its place a flower appeared, purple within, and surrounded with white leaves, which bears the name and preserves the memory of the handsome youth.

**The Princess of Seven Jasmines**

A king had an only son. Once, for some unknown reason, the kingdom was overrun by snakes and they caused a lot of havoc. The young prince decided to look into the matter himself and fight the snakes. One day, after hunting and killing hundreds of the snakes in the nearby forest, he rested under a tree and fell asleep. His servants were all around him.

Just then, a great big snake, a seven-hooded snake, began to descend from the branches of the tree the prince was sleeping under. The servants caught sight of it, drew their swords, and were about to cut it to pieces when the prince woke up and his eye fell on the seven-hooded snake above him. The snake looked at him, eye to eye, and there was a look of great pain in its eyes. The prince asked his servants to do nothing, but to step back. He addressed the snake directly.

"King of snakes, what do you want?" he asked gently. It replied in a human voice with human words.

"For seven long years I've had a terrible headache. I haven't been able to attend to my duties as a king and I haven't been able to discipline my subjects. They're running amok and creating havoc wherever they go."

"Can we do something about your headache? What's the cure?" The snake said,

"If you go seven leagues south of this forest, you'll come to another kingdom. The princess is an only daughter of the king there, and she is beautiful and delicate—she weighs only as much as seven blossoms of jasmine. She has never laughed, and when she does, three jasmine flowers will fall from her mouth. If you can bring the middle one of the three to me, and if I can smell its fragrance, my headache will vanish. Then, I promise you, I'll see to it your kingdom will never more be troubled by my snakes."

The prince said, "So it shall be," and set out that very day towards the southern regions. He sent word to his parents that he was going for such and such a job and asked them not to worry about him. As he travelled on, he came to a pool of clear water. He knelt by its bank to quench his thirst and his eye fell on a whole nest of ants that had fallen into the water. Even as they were struggling and drowning, he said, "Poor things!" and with his handkerchief he picked up the whole nest of ants and set them on dry ground. All of them survived. The king of ants was very pleased and grateful. He said to the prince, in the tiniest of voices,

"You did us a good turn. We'll never forget it. If you ever need us, think of us, and we'll be there to help you."

"That's great," said the prince, and bade them goodbye.

As he moved on, he heard a fearful, strange cry in the forest. He went in search of its source, and soon found himself in front of an enormous body, larger than anything he had ever seen before, lying in the middle of the road.

Apparently, some time ago, this giant had eaten his fill, almost to bursting, and had fallen asleep, snoring with his mouth open, when a crow flying in the sky with a tamarind fruit had dropped a seed right into his wide-open mouth. The tamarind seed had taken root and grown into a huge tree while he was still fast asleep. By the time the prince arrived on the scene, the giant had woken up, but he couldn't get up or move his mouth even, pinned under the weight of the tree that had grown up there. He was making strange crying and gurgling noises. The compassionate prince cut down the tree, and the giant was able to pull out the roots and the rest of it from his mouth.

The giant felt he was saved from a horrible death, and in his joy and gratitude he said to the prince,

"If you ever need help in anything, just think of me."

The prince said, "That's good, I certainly will," and moved on. He soon reached the very kingdom the seven-hooded snake had spoken about. There he sent word to the king that such and such a prince from such and such a kingdom had come to visit him and that he had come specially to marry the princess who weighed no more than seven jasmines. The king summoned him to his presence and was very pleased with the looks and manner of the visiting prince. He said,

"No one so far has had the courage to make this long journey and visit our kingdom. You look like someone special. But, if you really wish to marry my daughter, you'll have to succeed in the three tasks I'll set."

"Tell me what they are," said the prince.

"We'll pour and mix together a hundred sacks of rice and a hundred sacks of black gram and give the mixture to you. You must separate them by dawn."

The prince agreed to try, and the king's servants led him to a large room where a huge heap of rice and black gram lay all mixed together, and they left him there for the night. For a while he wondered what he could do, when he suddenly remembered the king of ants, who arrived with the speed of thought with his entire bustling entourage. Before the prince had told them what the task was, they had begun to work, and by morning they had separated the rice from the black gram and arranged them in two heaps. The king came to inspect the work of the prince in the morning, and said,

"Bravo! That's a man after my heart. The next thing you have to do is to eat. We'll give you a hundred and one portions of cooked rice and a hundred and one large measures of buttermilk. You'll have to mix them and eat all of it by morning."

As soon as they left him alone with the rice and the buttermilk, he thought of the giant, who arrived at once from nowhere, mixed the buttermilk and the rice, and ate it all up in just three mouthfuls. When the king came to see him in the morning, he was astonished.

"Terrific! You did that too. Now for the third task. Today our kingdom celebrates and worships Siva. There's a hill on the northern border and on it there's a big golden bell. You must go and ring that bell. It can be heard in all the seven kingdoms around here," said the king, and the prince replied,

"Sure, I'll leave for the hill of the golden bell this minute," and set out on his task.

When he got there and climbed the hill, he found a golden bell that was so large it looked like another hill on top of the first one. Ordinary mortals could not think of moving it. The prince thought again of the giant, who appeared at once and asked,

"What's the matter? You called me again."

"You must help me one more time, giant. Just pick up this bell and ring it just once. Then you can go."

"Is that all?" said the giant, picking up the golden bell and ringing it gleefully with all his might, till the seven kingdoms all around rang and shook with the sound of it.

The prince returned and was received with honours by the happy king, who was delighted at finding such a valiant son-in-law. He arranged a festive wedding at once and gave his daughter in marriage to him, loaded the newlyweds with hundreds of gifts, and gave them a splendid send-off with long processions of horses and elephants and all that.

As the prince was coming home with his new bride, the princess who weighed no more than seven jasmines, they ran into acrobats who were showing monkey-tricks with their trained monkeys. The princess, who had never left the four walls of her palace and was innocent of all experience and had never laughed even once, asked the prince what they were doing.

"O that, that's a monkey show. Let's go see it," said the prince.

"What's a monkey?" she asked in her innocence.

"See for yourself," said the prince, and took her by the hand and led her to the monkey show. She had never seen anything like it: monkeys that looked and acted like little men, somersaulted and walked and begged and played tricks on the audience. She began to laugh, and as she laughed, three divine jasmine flowers fell from her mouth. The prince picked up the middle one and put it safely in his pocket. On their way home, they stopped at the tree where he knew the seven-hooded serpent king would be waiting for him. As soon as the serpent king smelled the jasmine, his seven-year headache disappeared. He was very happy and, as a token of his appreciation, he gave the prince a snake-jewel and said,

"If you should ever need me, look into this jewel and think of me. I'll help you overcome any obstacle."

The prince saluted the serpent king and took his leave. By the time he came back to his kingdom, snakes no longer infested it. They were all gone, as if by miracle. The king, his father, was delighted to hear of his son's many adventures, and he arranged another gorgeous wedding in his capital for his son and his bride, the princess who weighed no more than seven jasmines.

**The Peony** (*Paeonia officinalis* cultivars)

That of necessity
it must be gathered in the night,
for if any man shall pluck
of the fruit in the daytime,
being seen of the woodpecker,
he is in danger to lose his eyes.
*Pliny*

The roots and seeds of the peony are considered to be magical. According to superstition, you should wear the seeds either strung or put a few loose seeds in your pocket to guard body spirit and soul. Another recommendation is to put cut branches in your home to ward off evil spirits. Peony is said to be named either after the Greek god of healing, Paeon, or after the physician Paeos, who cured Pluto and other gods of wounds received during the Trojan War with this plant.

This plant is thought to be of divine origin, an emanation from moonbeams. Peony was said to shine at night, protecting shepherds and their flocks. It is said to protect harvests, drive away evil spirits and avert storms.

It was believed that to pluck the peony up by the roots could cause danger to whoever touched it. A solution to the problem was to fasten a string to it in the night and to tie a hungry dog to the end of the string. By tempting the dog with scraps of food, it could be persuaded to pull on the string and so pluck the plant up for you.

The root was carried to cure 'lunacy'. The seeds placed on a 'lunatic' were said to cure the person of the affliction almost instantly. It was thought best to gather roots or seeds only at night, when the seeds are said to shine with an eerie glow. Peony roots can be carved into small beads that are called 'piney beads'. String them to wear for protection against evil - to stave off epilepsy, lunacy and nightmares. The seeds of the peony can also be added to wine as a remedy for nightmares.

**The Princess Peony**

Many years ago at Gamogun, in the province of Omi, was a castle called Adzuchi-no-shiro. It was a magnificent old place, surrounded by walls and a moat filled with lotus lilies. The feudal lord was a very brave and wealthy man, Yuki Naizen-no-jo. His wife had been dead for some years. He had no son; but he had a beautiful daughter aged eighteen, who (for some reason which is not quite clear to me) was given the title of Princess.

For a considerable period there had been peace and quiet in the land; the feudal lords were on the best of terms, and everyone was happy. Amid these circumstances Lord Naizen-no-jo perceived that there was a good opportunity to find a husband for his daughter Princess Aya; and after a time the second son of the Lord of Ako, of Harima Province, was selected, to the satisfaction of both fathers, the affair having little to do with the principals. Lord Ako's second son had viewed his bride with approval, and she him. One may say that young people are bound to approve each other when it is the parents' wish that they be united. Many suicides result from this.

Princess Aya made her mind up to try and love her prospective husband. She saw nothing of him; but she thought of him, and talked of him.

One evening when Princess Aya was walking in the magnificent gardens by the moonlight, accompanied by her maids-in-waiting, she wandered down through her favourite peony bed to the pond where she loved to gaze at her reflection on the nights of the full moon, to listen to frogs, and to watch the fireflies.

When nearing the pond her foot slipped, and she would have fallen into the water had it not been that a young man appeared as if by magic and caught her. He disappeared as soon as he had put her on her feet again.

The maids-of-honour saw her slip; they saw a glimmer of light, and that was all. But Princess Aya had seen more. She had seen the handsomest young man she could imagine.

"Twenty-one years old," she said to O Sadayo San, her favourite maid, "he must have been -- a samurai of the highest order. His dress was covered with my favourite peonies, and his swords were richly mounted. Oh that I could have seen him a minute longer, to thank him for saving me from the water! Who can he be? And how could he have got into our gardens, through all the guards?"

So spoke the princess to her maids, directing them at the same time that they were to say a word to no one, for fear that her father should hear, find the young man, and behead him for trespass.

After this evening Princess Aya fell sick. She could not eat or sleep, and turned pale. The day for her marriage with the young Lord of Ako came and went without the event; she was far too sick for that. The best of the doctors had been sent from Kyoto, which was then the capital; but none of them had been able to do anything, and the maid grew thinner and thinner.

As a last resource, the Lord Naizen-no-jo, her father, sent for her most confidential maid and friend, O Sadayo, and demanded if she could give any reason for his daughter's mysterious sickness. Had she a secret lover? Had she a particular dislike for her betrothed?

"Sir," said O Sadayo, "I do not like to tell secrets; but here it seems my duty to your lordship's daughter as well as to your lordship. Some three weeks ago, when the moon was at its full, we were walking in the peony beds down near the pond where the princess loves to be. She stumbled and nearly fell into the water, when a strange thing happened. In an instant a most beautiful young samurai appeared and helped her up, thus preventing her from falling into the pond. We could all see the glimmer of him; but your daughter and I saw him most distinctly. Before your daughter could thank him he had disappeared. None of us could understand how it was possible for a man to get into the gardens of the princess, for the gates of the castle are guarded on all sides, and the princess's garden is so much better guarded than the rest that it seems truly incredible that a man could get in. We maids were asked to say nothing for fear of your lordship's anger. Since that evening it is that our beloved princess Aya has been sick, sir. It is sickness of the heart. She is deeply in love with the young samurai she saw for so brief a space. Indeed, my lord, there never was such a handsome man in the world before, and if we cannot find him the young princess, I fear, will die."

"How is it possible for a man to get into the grounds?" said Lord Yuki Naizen-no-jo. "People say foxes and badgers assume the figures of men sometimes; but even so it is impossible for such supernatural beings to enter my castle grounds, guarded as it is at every opening."

That evening the poor princess was more wearily unhappy than ever before. Thinking to enliven her a little, the maids sent for a celebrated player on the biwa, called Yashaskita Kengyo. The weather being hot, they were sitting on the gallery (engawa); and while the musician was playing "Dannoura" there appeared suddenly from behind the peonies the same handsome young samurai. He was visible to all this time -- even the peonies embroidered on his dress.

"There he is! There he is!" they cried; at which he instantly disappeared again. The princess was highly excited, and seemed more lively than she had been for days; the old Daimio grew more puzzled than ever when he heard of it.

Next night, while two of the maids were playing for their mistress -- O Yae San the flute, and O Yakumo the koto -- the figure of the young man appeared again.

A thorough search having been made during the day in the immense peony beds with absolutely no result, not even the sign of a footmark, the thing was increasingly strange.

A consultation was held, and it was decided by the lord of the castle to invite a veteran officer of great strength and renown, Maki Hiogo, to capture the youth should he appear that evening. Maki Hiogo readily consented, and at the appointed time, dressed in black and consequently invisible, concealed himself among the peonies.

Music seemed to have a fascination for the young samurai. It was while music was being played that he had made his appearances. Consequently, O Yae and O Yakumo resumed their concert, while all gazed eagerly towards the peony beds. As the ladies played a piece called

"Sofuren," there, sure enough, arose the figure of a young samurai, dressed magnificently in clothes which were covered with embroidered peonies.

Everyone gazed at him, and wondered why Maki Hiogo did not jump up and catch him. The fact was that Maki Hiogo was so much astonished by the noble bearing of the youth that at first he did not want to touch him. Recovering himself, and thinking of his duty to his lord, he stealthily approached the young man, and, seizing him round the waist, held him tight. After a few seconds Maki Hiogo felt a kind of wet steam falling on his face; by degrees it made him faint; and he fell to the ground, still grasping the young samurai, for he had made up his mind that he would secure him.

Everyone had seen the scuffle, and some of the guards came hurrying to the place. Just as they reached the spot Maki Hiogo came to his senses, and shouted,

"Come, gentlemen! I have caught him. Come and see!" But on looking at what he held in his arms he discovered it to be only a large peony! By this time the Lord Naizen-no-jo had arrived at the spot where Maki Hiogo lay, and so had the Princess Aya and her maids.

All were astounded and mystified except the Daimio himself, who said "Ah! It is as I said. No fox or badger spirit could pass our guards and get into this garden. It is the spirit of the peony flower that took the form of a prince." Turning to his daughter and her maids, he said,

"You must take this a compliment, and pay great respect to the peony, and show the one caught by Maki Hiogo kindness as well by taking care of it."

The Princess Aya carried the flower back to her room, where she put it in a vase of water and placed it near her pillow. She felt as if she had her sweetheart with her. Day by day she got better. She tended the peony herself, and, strange to say, the flower seemed to get stronger and stronger, instead of fading. At last the princess recovered. She became radiantly beautiful, while the peony continued to remain in perfect bloom, showing no sign of dying.

The Princess Aya being now perfectly well, her father could no longer put off the wedding. Consequently, some days later, the Lord of Ako and his family arrived at the castle, and his second son was married to the princess.

As soon as the wedding was over the peony was found still in its vase -- but dead and withered. The villagers always after this, instead of speaking of the Princess Aya, or Aya Hime, called her Botan Hime or Peony Princess.[4]

---

4 The tale was found in a collection by Richard Gordon Smith, *Ancient Tales and Folklore of Japan* (London: A. and C. Black, 1908)

**The Iris** (*Iris sp.*)

Iris is the Greek word for rainbow. It is also the name of the ancient Greek goddess of the rainbow. The goddess Iris used the arc of the rainbow to slide messages from the gods down to earth. One of the duties of the Greek Goddess Iris was to lead the souls of dead women to the Elysian Fields. In token of that faith the Greeks planted purple Iris on the graves of women. The Iris played a part in ancient Egyptian ritual as well. The Iris flower represented strength and power to the Egyptians. Iris flowers were used to adorn the sceptres of the pharaohs and were also placed on the brow of the sphinx.

Most legends of how the iris came to represent the French monarchy centre around two historical incidents. The first involves Clovis, who in 496 A.D. is said to have abandoned the three toads on his banner in favour of the fleur-de-lis. His Christian Queen Clotilda, had long sought to convert her heathen husband but he always ignored her plea. Then faced with a formidable army of Alamanni (the Germanic tribe invading his kingdom) he told his wife that if he won the battle he would admit her God was strongest and be baptized. He did win and the toads disappeared. The second incident occurred in 1147. Louis VII of France had a dream that convinced him to adopt the purple iris as his device shortly before setting out for his ill-fated crusade. This is how the fleur-de-lis became the symbol of the monarchy.

The Iris became such a powerful symbol of the French kings that the Revolutionaries in 1789 set out to totally obliterate it - by having it chipped off buildings and torn from draperies. Men were even guillotined for wearing a fleur-de-lis on their clothes or as jewellery.

For a long time orris root was responsible for making social interaction bearable. It was used as a perfume for linen and is mentioned in 1480 in the wardrobe accounts of Edward IV. Several pieces of dried orris root strung on a string would be plunged into the boiling water with the clothes. In those times people wore wool or if they were important silk, satin or velvet. There were no dry cleaners then so ‘Swete cloth’ underneath the clothes and a great deal of perfume on top was the best to be done, since bathing was considered dangerous by physicians in those days.

**The Shepherd and the Iris**

Once upon a time there was a young and handsome shepherd who loved his job very much. One day, while watching his sheep, he began to play the long pipe so beautifully that even the birds were listening to him.

Not far from there Luck was having an argument with Mind:

"I'm bigger and more important than you!" Luck said angrily.

"No, I'm bigger and more important than you!" Mind replied defiantly. And so they carried on, continuing to argue about who was more important, with neither of them being prepared to give in.

"Shall we have a contest?" Mind said.

"Yes. That way we can settle this once and for all!" Luck replied.

"Good" Mind said. "Look at that shepherd over there. Go down and visit him. I'll vacate his head and then you have the chance to show me what you can do". Luck agreed to the challenge and so the contest commenced.

The shepherd got up and found a pile of money, but lacking mind, he wanted to feed the sheep with it. But the poor sheep needed to eat and to drink water. Then he had another idea. Seeing that the coins made a noise, he thought of hanging them on the rams' horns. Then he left for the town to sell them because he felt like eating pumpkin.

On his way he met a merchant. The merchant, who was a bad man, persuaded the shepherd to sell him the rams for a loaf of bread, a pumpkin and bed for a night in his house. Chatting with him, the shepherd began to talk about his good luck and the rest of the money he had found. When he heard this, the merchant befriended the shepherd, took him to his place, bought him new clothes and walked together with him through the yard every day.

Now in front of the merchant's house stood the Emperor's palace and the Emperor became very curious to find out who the new arrival was. The merchant introduced the shepherd to the Emperor, telling him that he was the son of a foreign emperor who had come to woo his daughter. The Emperor was very glad to hear that and made the necessary preparations for the wedding. They had a great feast that lasted three weeks. But when the shepherd went with his bride in their room, he started to play the long pipe as if he were with his sheep, instead of spending the time with his new wife. Hearing that, the Emperor ordered him to be hanged.

Then the time came for Mind to return and Luck to leave. The shepherd begged the Emperor to forgive him, but the Emperor was merciless. Seeing that there was no chance of being forgiven, he opened his big mouth and started to think of God. Feeling pity for him, God turned him into a flower like that, with a wide open mouth, and the flower became known as an Iris.

**The Crocus** (*Crocus sativus*)

In mythology, Crocus was a friend of the Greek God Hermes. While playing one day, Hermes accidentally killed Crocus and a small flower grew at the site.

Three drops of Crocus' blood fell on the flower, creating the spots often seen on the crocus. In a related myth, Crocus was a young man who transformed into the crocus flower because of his unfulfilled love for a nymph named Smilax.

Crocuses flower around Valentine's Day. *Krokos* was the Greek name for the saffron crocus. It was considered to be an aphrodisiac. The legend about its origin is of Zeus and Hera making love so passionately that the heat of their ardour made the bank they were lying on burst open with crocuses. Another legend says that Krokos was accidentally killed by Mercury during a game of quoits and that a saffron-bearing flower sprang from the ground where Krokos bled.

*Crocologia*, published in 1670, was devoted to the medicinal properties of the plant. In 19th century England, saffron was used as an aromatic. Saffron concoctions were designed to raise the spirits and the herb was reputed to move men to laughter.

From earliest times, the best quality saffron came from Cilicia, in the Persian Empire (Iran). Crocuses grown in Spain produce the best quality saffron too. It is one of the sweet-smelling herbs in the Bible (Song of Solomon 4:14.) and it has a long history of spiritual and magical use. It is an ancient symbol of the sun and has been used to dye foods the colour yellow as part of solar worship. Mice and rats love the flowers, squirrels dig them up and birds love to peck the petals off.

In India saffron is used in many recipes for rice and sweets. It is used in Ayurvedic medicine and in religious rituals too. In Saudi Arabia, real Arabic coffee has saffron and cardamom added to give it a unique flavour. It is essential in the preparation of risotto and an indispensable ingredient in *paella* too.

**How the Crocus got its Fur Coat**

To enter the world of chiefs Wapee, son of a chief, was to spend four days and nights on top of a lonely hill until a vision of the man he was to be came to him. The first night, no visions appeared to him and he was downhearted. But with the dawn, the warming sun beamed upon a beautiful flower who opened her petals and nodded towards Wapee as if to welcome him. Wapee no longer felt alone.

When night came again, Wapee curled his body around his new friend to protect her from the icy night winds. Three times he did this and three times when the Morning Star rose, visions came to him foretelling of great things to come. When Wapee rose to leave he said:

"You have comforted and counselled me well these past three days and nights. What three wishes would you have me ask of the Great Spirit?"

"Pray that I may have the purple blue of the distant mountains in my petals, a small golden sun to hold close to my heart on dull days, and a furry coat to face the cold winds in the spring."

The Great Spirit was so pleased with Wapee's thoughtfulness, that he gave him everything he asked for and made sure all his dreams came true.

**The Dandelion** (*Taraxacum officinale*)

It is the resemblance of the distinctive leaves to the canine teeth of a lion that is said to have given the plant its name, which is a corruption of the French Dent de Lion, an equivalent of this name being found not only in its former specific Latin name, *Dens leonis*, but also in the Greek name for the genus to which Linnaeus assigned it, *Leontodon*. The name of the genus, Taraxacum, is derived from the Greek *taraxos* (disorder), and *akos* (remedy), on account of the curative action of the plant.

The dandelion takes an important place among honey-producing plants, as it furnishes considerable quantities of both pollen and nectar in the early spring, when the bees' harvest from fruit trees is nearly over. It is also important from the beekeeper's point of view, because not only does it flower most in spring, no matter how cool the weather may be, but a small succession of bloom is also kept up until late autumn, so that it is a source of honey after the main flowers have ceased to bloom, thus delaying the need for feeding the colonies of bees with artificial food.

A very noticeable feature of the dandelion is the silky whiteness of the plant's large gossamer ball. It is made up of myriads of plumed seeds or pappus, ready to be blown off when quite ripe by the slightest breeze, and forms the 'clock' of the children, who by blowing at it till all the seeds are released, love to tell themselves the time of day by the number of puffs necessary to disperse every seed.

Dandelion leaves can be blanched in the same way as endive and used in salads. The roots can also be used in salads or as vegetables in spring or autumn. Dandelion leaves are very high in vitamins A, B, C, and D. The A content in dandelion leaves is higher than that of carrots. Dandelion flowers are used to make a wonderful country wine and the roots provide a healthy alternative to coffee when dried, chopped and roasted. Dandelion 'mushrooms' can be prepared by covering the rinsed moist flowers in flour, heating butter in a heavy frying pan, then adding the flowers and frying quickly, turning them to brown all sides.

**The Love of the South Wind for the Dandelion**

Shawondasee, the south wind, heavy, drowsy, lazy, likes to lie in the shade of live oaks and magnolias, inhaling the scent of blossoms and filling his lungs so full of it that when he breathes again you detect the perfume.

One day Shawondasee, gazing over his fields with a sleepy eye, saw at a distance a slender girl with yellow hair. He admired her, and but for his heaviness he would even have called her to his side. Next morning he looked again, and she was still there, more beautiful than ever. Every day he looked, and his eye sparkled when he saw the maid in the warm green prairie. But one morning he rubbed his eyes and looked hard a second time, for he did not trust them at first: a woman was standing where the maid had been at sundown, but what a change! The youth was gone, the brightness fled. Instead of a crown of golden glory, here was a faded creature and her hair looked grey.

"Ah," sighed Shawondasee, "my brother, the North Wind, has been here in the night. He has put his cruel hand upon her head, and whitened it with frost." Shawondasee put out such a mighty sigh that it reached the spot where the girl had stood, and behold! Her white hair fell from her head, tossed off upon that breath, and she was gone. Others like her came, and the earth is glad with them; but in the spring Shawondasee sighs unceasingly for the maiden with the yellow hair as he first saw her.[5]

---

5 The Algonquin legend above has been adapted from a story in *Myths and Legends of Flowers, Trees, Fruits, and Plants*, by Charles M. Skinner, c. 1911 published by J.B. Lippincott Company.

# Chapter 12
# FIVE EXAMPLES OF PARABLES

A parable can be defined as a short tale that illustrates a universal truth. It sketches a setting, describes an action, and shows the results. It often involves a character facing a moral dilemma, or making a questionable decision and then suffering the consequences. As with a fable, a parable generally relates a single, simple, consistent action, without extraneous detail or distracting circumstances. Fables use animals, plants, inanimate objects, and forces of nature as characters, though, while parables generally feature people.

Aside from providing guidance and suggestions for proper action in life, parables frequently use metaphorical language which allows people to more easily discuss difficult or complex ideas. In Plato's *Republic*, parables like the 'Parable of the Cave' (in which the understanding of truth is presented as a story about being deceived by shadows on the wall of a cave) teach an abstract argument, using a concrete narrative which is more easily grasped.

Parables are often used to express of spiritual concepts. A source of parables in Christianity is the Gospels section of the New Testament, where examples include 'the Good Samaritan' and 'the Prodigal Son'. Examples from the *Old Testament* include the "parable of the ewe-lamb" told by Nathan in 2 Samuel 12:1-9, and that of 'the woman of Tekoah' in 2 Samuel 14:1-13. In the Sufi tradition, parables ('teaching stories') are also used for imparting lessons and values, and modern stories can of course be used as parables too.

*Read the following parable, and then decide what the missing word in the title is:*

**It's all in the _____**

The wife of a man became very sick. On her deathbed, she said to him,

"I love you so much! I don't want to leave you, and I don't want you to betray me. Promise that you will not see any other women once I die, or I will come back to haunt you."

For several months after her death, the husband did avoid other women, but then he met someone and fell in love. On the night that they were engaged to be married, the ghost of his former wife appeared to him. She blamed him for not keeping the promise, and every night thereafter she returned to taunt him. The ghost would remind him of everything that transpired between him and his fiancé that day, even to the point of repeating, word for word, their conversations. It upset him so badly that he couldn't sleep at all.

Desperate, he sought the advice of a Zen master who lived near the village.

"This is a very clever ghost," the master said upon hearing the man's story.

"It is!" replied the man. "She remembers every detail of what I say and do. It knows everything!" The master smiled,

"You should admire such a ghost, but I will tell you what to do the next time you see it."

That night the ghost returned. The man responded just as the master had advised.

"You are such a wise ghost," the man said, "You know that I can hide nothing from you. If you can answer me one question, I will break off the engagement and remain single for the rest of my life."

"Ask your question," the ghost replied. The man scooped up a handful of beans from a large bag on the floor,

"Tell me exactly how many beans there are in my hand."

At that moment the ghost disappeared and never returned.

**How Tamerlane found his Fortune**

One day Temir, whose horse was lame and had lost his son, called on a blacksmith. At that time the blacksmith was sleeping, and Temir, not wanting to disturb him, sat down by his side, waiting for him to wake up. He noticed that a fly came out of the blacksmith's nose, crawled along the tongs across a basin to the anvil. Beyond the anvil there was a huge fissure; the fly descended into this fissure and remained there quite a long time. Then it crawled back out and, after passing the anvil, crossed the basin by the same tongs, but while crossing it fell into the water. For a long time it was struggling in the water, but eventually it somehow managed to crawl out of the basin, and went back into the nose of the blacksmith again.

"It seems I've been asleep for quite some time!"

"Yes, and I've been sitting waiting all that time". Temir replied. "Amuse me. I've lost my son, my horse has pulled up lame and I've really had enough of everything today. Tell me something to take my mind off things and to cheer me up a bit."

"But what can I tell you?" The blacksmith answered. After all, nobody can ever possibly obtain what I've just seen in my dream, and it would just make you even more frustrated". Temir asked him, nevertheless, to relate what he had experienced, and so the blacksmith did.

"In my dream I crossed a big river and an iron mountain and went down into a large cave, where there was treasure of gold and silver; for a long time I stood there, not having the strength to tear my eyes away from the brilliance and the splendour. But being conscious that I had to return, I climbed out of the cave. On the return journey when I was crossing the river, I fell off the bridge and almost drowned".

It was then Temir realised that it was the soul of the blacksmith which had come out in the form of a fly. And guessing that there had to be some great treasure in the smithy, he persuaded the blacksmith to give the place up to him. Then after digging up the very same spot where the soul of the blacksmith had crawled, Temir exposed untold wealth, with which he collected an army and subjugated the whole world.[6]

*What this traditional folktale shows is the ancient Ingush (from Ingushetia in the Caucasus) belief in the reality of dreams and how the soul for them was something material rather than an abstract spiritual concept. In fact, what it reflects is an understanding of the soul that is remarkably similar to that of the Siberian Buryats. There is even a parallel Buryat tale in which the soul takes the form of a bee when it crawls out of someone's nose for an out-of-body experience (see Dalgat, 2004, p.40).*

**Reference:**

Dalgat, B.K. (2004) *The Aboriginal Religions of the Chechens and Ingush*, Moscow: NAUKA. (Translated from the Russian by David Hunt October 2009, and kept in the British Library. The book was first published in an abridged form in 1893).

6 (Adapted from Dalgat, 2004, p.39-40).

## The After-Life, and the Banquet of the King

There was a certain king who made a feast and invited everyone in his kingdom to it; but he made a decree that every man should bring with him something to sit upon at the feast. Some brought with them beautiful and comfortable cushions, some brought handsome but hard seats, some brought sofas to recline upon, some brought logs of wood, and some brought stones and boulders. The king provided everything for the nourishment and entertainment of all comers, and to adorn the court of the palace; but ordered that each man should sit, at the feast, on the couch or seat that he had made or brought for himself.

Then they who were sitting on logs, and stones, and other uncomfortable and ugly seats, grumbled at the king and said:

"Is it to the honour of the king that we should be sitting here in such discomfort, on nothing but stones and old bits of wood?" And when the king heard their complaints he said to them,

"Is it not enough for you that you disgrace my palace with stones and logs, my palace that I have built and beautified at so much cost; but will you also insult me by suggesting I'm to blame for the predicament you now find yourselves in? The truth of the matter is that your honour and splendour, all that you have, is nothing more and nothing less than exactly what you've made for yourselves." [7]

## The Peacemaker

It is reported that two kingdoms were on the verge of war for the possession of a certain embankment which was disputed by them. And the Buddha, seeing the kings and their armies ready to fight requested them to tell him the cause of their quarrels. Having heard the complaints on both sides, he said,

"I understand that the embankment has value for some of your people; has it any intrinsic value aside from its service to your men?"

"It has no intrinsic value whatever", was the reply. The Tathagata continued:

"Now when you go to battle is it not sure that many of your men will be slain and that you yourselves, O kings, are liable to lose your lives?" And they said:

---

7 This parable has been adapted from *The Wisdom of Israel: Extracts from the Babylonian Talmud and Midrash Rabboth.* Translated form the Aramaic and Hebrew, with an Introduction by Edwin Collins London: John Murray (1910).

"It is sure that many will be slain and our own lives jeopardized too."

"The blood of men, however," said Buddha, "has it less intrinsic value than a mound of earth?"

"No," the kings said, "The lives of men and above all the lives of kings, are priceless." Then the Tathagata concluded:

"Care you going to stake that which is priceless against that which has no intrinsic value whatever?"

The wrath of the two monarchs abated, and they came to a peaceable agreement.[8]

*Read the following parable, and then decide what the missing word in the title is:*

**The Importance of _____**

A man was sitting in his house one night, and the rain was just pouring outside. On TV he heard that there was flooding in the area.

He said, "I'm not worried, God will save me."

He woke up the next morning and found that the nearby river had overflowed and flooded his entire house. He could not even go downstairs because the water had risen above the first floor. As he looked out his second story window a man in a rowing boat happened to pass by, and he yelled, "Jump in! I'll save you!"

"No, thank you," said the man, "God will save me."

The water continued to rise, and the man climbed up onto the roof. Another boat with two men in it then passed by. One of the men yelled, "Get in! We'll save you!"

Again, the man replied, "No, thank you. God will save me."

The man was on his roof, water to his waist, praying for a miracle. A helicopter flew by this time and dropped a rope. "Grab on, and I'll pull you up", the pilot yelled.

8 *Buddha, the Gospel*, by Paul Carus. Chicago: The Open Court Publishing Company, 1894, and is in the public domain.

“No, thanks,” the man answered, “God will save me”.

After a few more minutes of trying to stay afloat the man was swept away and drowned. When he arrived in heaven, the man asked to see God. When he was brought before him he said, “Tell me Lord, what happened? I had faith in you. I prayed for a miracle, over and over again. So why didn’t you save me then?”

The Lord replied, “What more do you want from me? I sent two boats and a helicopter!”

## Chapter 13
## THE ENDLESS JOURNEY

When we leave home and set out on our journeys through life, most of us have expectations. However, for all the meticulous planning that frequently takes place, we can never be sure where we might eventually end up. This is what can make life such a joy or a headache - the unexpected twists and turns of fate we encounter along the way. In the contemporary tale that starts this journey, you can be sure that the pedigree champion bred to win Crufts never expected to end up where he did. Although it might not have been the life his breeder had anticipated for him, it certainly proved to be an interesting adventure, and although Pushkin might never have become the champion he was supposed to have become, all the love he received more than compensated for that:

**The Shopkeeper's Nightmare**

She could keep at it for hours on end. All she needed was the occasional break and then she'd be at it again, with just the same enthusiasm as when she first started - shopping, I mean. But she didn't actually buy anything. It was nearly always window shopping - comparing quality and prices, trying things on to see how they fitted, then calculating how much she would save to send her children by not buying the items she fancied.

You see, she didn't earn very much. And what she did earn was saved to send home to her children. Every penny she spent on herself was a penny less for them. And it was mainly out of consideration for them and her bedridden father that she'd come to England in the first place, to provide them with a better future. She'd joined a dating agency called Russian Brides that specialised in finding wives for Western misfits.

However, eventually the temptation became too great. She made up her mind to buy the children something she had always dreamed of owning but never been able to back home. Something way out of her price range, a total extravagance, a pedigree dog, that nobody else back home could ever afford to have.

Everyone around her told her it was utter madness and there were more important things to spend her money on - medicine for her father, for example. However, being a stubborn character, the more they tried to convince her of the error of her ways, the more determined she became.

The particular breed she wanted was only available in Manchester but she couldn't afford to spend the money on the train and still have enough to pay for the dog. However, one of her compatriots hired a car to take her up there for the day. Not that it did him much good. Because despite her shortcomings, she would never dream of being unfaithful to the man she'd given up her home to be with. As for him, he wasn't prepared to help her at all in her efforts. He was just waiting for her to fail so that he could say *I told you so.*

Anyway, despite all the difficulties, eventually she got the puppy. But the story didn't end there. She was a dreamer by nature and paid little attention to practical considerations such as how to transport the animal back home and all the official papers required. It turned out the only way was to travel back home with the dog herself. However, she missed her connection in Geneva and had to spend the night there with the animal.

The airline company compensated her by putting her up in a five star hotel, where she was treated like Royalty, until an onward flight was available. The dog was given his own special basket and dined in the restaurant with a choice of menu served in a silver bowl. And he wasn't ungrateful for all the kindness bestowed on him. He showed his appreciation by leaving a token of his affection in the middle of the hotel lobby. The staff cleared it away with the utmost professionalism, acting as if nothing untoward had happened, as if it was something they dealt with every day of their lives. But secretly they must have been mightily relieved to learn of their odd guest's imminent departure.

As for the dog, whose name was Pushkin, it eventually reached its new home, a dilapidated tower block in a former Soviet Republic, where it lived on whatever scraps were available. It was a far cry from the pedigree diet recommended by the breeder and hardly suitable fare for the son of a seven time Champion at Cruft's. But he did have what no amount of money could ever buy - unlimited love and attention. And she had succeeded in proving her critics wrong even though it had cost her an arm and a leg.

*In the next story, it is a scorpion that decides to go on a journey. The frog bravely puts his faith in the fact that people are basically good, and that even proven killers can change their natures. However, to find out whether his trust is misguided or not you will have to read the tale!*

**The Scorpion and the Frog**

One day, a scorpion looked around at the mountain where he lived and decided that he wanted a change. So he set out on a journey through the forests and hills. He climbed over rocks and under vines and kept going until he reached a river.

The river was wide and swift, and the scorpion stopped to reconsider the situation. He couldn't see any way across. So he ran upriver and then checked downriver, all the while thinking that he might have to turn back.

Suddenly, he saw a frog sitting in the rushes by the bank of the stream on the other side of the river. He decided to ask the frog for help to get across.

"Hellooo Mr. Frog!" called the scorpion across the water, "Would you be so kind as to give me a ride on your back across the river?"

"Well now, Mr. Scorpion! How do I know that if I try to help you, you won't try to *kill* me?" asked the frog hesitantly.

"Because," the scorpion replied, "If I tried to kill you, then I'd die too, for you see I can't swim!"

Now this seemed to make sense to the frog. But he asked. "What about when I get close to the bank? You could still try to kill me and get back to the shore!"

"That's true," agreed the scorpion, "But then I wouldn't be able to get to the other side of the river!"

"Alright then...how do I know you won't just wait till we get to the other side and then kill me?" said the frog.

"Ahh...," crooned the scorpion, "Because you see, once you took me to the other side of this river, I'd be so grateful for your help, that it would hardly be fair to reward you with death, now would it?!"

So the frog agreed to take the scorpion across the river. He swam over to the bank and settled himself near the mud to pick up his passenger. The scorpion crawled onto the frog's back, his sharp claws prickling into the frog's soft hide, and the frog slid into the river. The muddy water swirled around them, but the frog stayed near the surface so the scorpion would not drown. He kicked strongly through the first half of the stream, his flippers paddling wildly against the current.

Halfway across the river, the frog suddenly felt a sharp sting in his back and, out of the corner of his eye, saw the scorpion remove his stinger from the frog's back. A deadening numbness began to creep into his limbs.

"You fool!" croaked the frog, "Now we'll both die! Why on earth did you do that?"

The scorpion shrugged did a little jig on the drowning frog's back, and replied:

"I couldn't help myself. It's my nature."

Then they both sank into the muddy waters of the swiftly flowing river.

Self destruction -

"It's my Nature", said the Scorpion.

*Here is another version of the same tale, in which it is the frog that decides to go on the journey. The character of the scorpion in the previous tale is replaced by a crocodile, but the result remains just the same:*

**The Frog and the Crocodile**

Once, there was a frog who lived in the middle of a swamp. His entire family had lived in that swamp for generations, but this particular frog decided that *he* had had quite enough wetness to last him a lifetime. He decided that he was going to find a dry place to live instead.

The only thing that separated him from dry land was a swampy, muddy, swiftly flowing river. But the river was home to all sorts of slippery, slithering snakes that loved nothing better than a good, plump frog for dinner, and Frog didn't dare try to swim across.

So for many days, the frog stayed put, hopping along the bank, trying to think of a way to get across.

The snakes hissed and jeered at him, daring him to come closer, but he refused. Occasionally they would slither closer, jaws open to attack, but the frog always leaped out of the way. But no matter how far upstream he searched or how far downstream, the frog wasn't able to find a way across the water.

He had felt certain that there would be a bridge, or a place where the banks came together, yet all he found was more reeds and water. After a while, even the snakes stopped teasing him and went off in search of easier prey.

The frog sighed in frustration and sat to sulk in the rushes. Suddenly, he spotted two big eyes staring at him from the water. The giant log-shaped animal opened its mouth and asked him, "What are you doing, Frog? Surely there are enough flies right there for a meal."

The frog croaked in surprise and leaped away from the crocodile. That creature could swallow him whole in a moment without thinking about it! Once he was a satisfied that he was a safe distance away, he answered. "I'm tired of living in swampy waters, and I want to travel to the other side of the river. But if I swim across, the snakes will eat me."

The crocodile harrumphed in agreement and sat, thinking, for a while. "Well, if you're afraid of the snakes, I could give you a ride across," he suggested.

"Oh no, I don't think so," Frog answered quickly. "You'd eat me on the way over, or go underwater so the snakes could get me!"

"Now why would I let the snakes get you? I think they're a terrible nuisance with all their hissing and slithering! The river would be much better off without them altogether! Anyway, if you're so worried that I might eat you, you can ride on my tail."

The frog considered his offer. He did want to get to dry ground very badly, and there didn't seem to be any other way across the river. He looked at the crocodile from his short, squat buggy eyes and wondered about the crocodile's motives. But if he rode on the tail, the croc couldn't eat him anyway. And he was right about the snakes - no self-respecting crocodile would give a meal to the snakes.

"Okay, it sounds like a good plan to me. Turn around so I can hop on your tail."

The crocodile flopped his tail into the marshy mud and let the frog climb on, then he waddled out to the river. But he couldn't stick his tail into the water as a rudder because the frog was on it -- and if he put his tail in the water, the snakes would eat the frog. They clumsily floated downstream that way for a while, until the crocodile said, "Hop onto my back so I can steer straight with my tail." The frog moved, and the journey smoothed out.

From where he was sitting, the frog couldn't see much except the back of Crocodile's head. "Why don't you hop up on my head so you can see everything around us?" Crocodile invited.

"But I don't want to see anything else," the frog answered, suddenly feeling nervous.

"Oh, come now. It's a beautiful view! Surely you don't think that I'm going to eat you after we're halfway across. My home is in the marsh - what would be the point of swimming across the river full of snakes if I didn't leave you on the other bank?"

Frog *was* curious about what the river looked like, so he climbed on top of Crocodile's head. The river looked almost pretty from this view. He watched dragonflies darting over the water and smiled in anticipation as he saw firm ground beyond the cattails. When the crocodile got close enough, the frog would leap off his head towards freedom. He wouldn't give the croc a chance to eat him.

"My nose tickles," the crocodile complained suddenly, breaking into the frog's train of thought. "I think there might be a fly buzzing around it somewhere."

"I don't see a fly," the frog said, peering at the crocodile's green snout. It seemed odd that anything could tickle a crocodile through its thick skin.

"Would you get rid of it for me?" the crocodile begged, twitching his nose. "I'm afraid I'll sneeze and send you flying. I don't want to feed you to the snakes."

The bank isn't too far, the frog thought. And it's the least he could do to repay him for bringing him over. So he hopped onto the crocodile's snout and checked the nostrils. Just a little closer, and he could jump... "I don't see -" he began.

Just then, with a terrific chomp the frog disappeared. The crocodile licked his lips in satisfaction. "Good, I feel much better already," he smiled, and turned around to go back home again.

*Now for a tale that comes from the Mbaka tribe, part of the Ambundu people of northwest Angola. It is retold from Folk-Tales of Angola, collected and edited by Heli Chatelain, (Houghton Mifflin, Boston and New York, 1894). The message is a positive one - remove the word can't from your vocabulary and everything then becomes possible!*

**How Frog went to Heaven**

Once upon a time there was a young man called Kimana. He wanted to marry the Sky Maiden so he wrote a letter to her father, the Sun Chief.

Kimana went to Rabbit. "Will you take this letter for me?"

Rabbit said, "I can't go to Heaven."

Kimana went to Antelope. "Will you take this letter for me?"

Antelope said, "I can't go to Heaven."

Kimana went to Hawk. "Will you take this letter for me?"

Hawk said, "I can go halfway to Heaven, but not all the way."

Then Frog came to Kimana. "Why don't you take the letter yourself?"

Kimana said, "This I can't do."

Frog said, "Then I'll take it for you."

Kimana laughed. "How can a frog take a letter to Heaven?"

Frog said, "Whatever it is, I can do it. But only if I try."

Now, Frog lived by a well. Every day, the girls who served the Sun Chief came to this well. They climbed down from Heaven on a web made by Spider. Then they filled their water jugs and went home.

Frog put the letter in his mouth and hid in the well. The girls from Heaven came for water, laughing and singing. They lowered their jugs into the well, and Frog jumped into one. The girls did not see.

Then the girls climbed back up the web of Spider. They went into the house of the Sun Chief and left the jugs in a room.

Frog was alone. He jumped out of the jug and spit the letter out on a bench. Then he hid in a corner.

The Sun Chief came for a drink of water. He saw the letter and opened it. He read, "I, Kimana, a man of earth, wish to marry the Sky Maiden, your daughter."

The Sun Chief said, "How can this be?"

He went to the girls who fetched water. "Did you bring this letter?"

The girls said, "No, we didn't."

He went to his wife, the Moon Lady, and read it to her. "What should we do?"

The Moon Lady said, "Don't ask me! Ask your daughter!"

He went to his daughter. The Sky Maiden said, "Let's see if he can bring a wedding gift."

So the Sun Chief wrote a letter and left it lying on the bench. Then he went away.

Frog came out and put the letter in his mouth. Then he climbed into an empty jug.

The next day, the girls took the jugs and climbed down to earth, laughing and singing. They lowered their jugs into the well, and Frog jumped out. The girls did not see. Then the girls went back to Heaven.

Frog took the letter to Kimana, and Kimana read it. "You may marry my daughter if you bring a purse of money."

Kimana said, "This I can't do."

Frog said, "Then I'll take it for you."

Kimana laughed. "I know you took a letter to Heaven but how can you take a purse of money?"

Frog said, "Whatever it is, I can do it. But only if I try."

Kimana gave Frog a purse of money. Frog took hold of it with his mouth and carried it to the well. He climbed in and waited.

The girls from Heaven came to the well. Frog got into one of the jugs. The girls returned to Heaven and left him in the room.

Frog set the money on the bench. Then he hid.

The Sun Chief came and found the purse. "How can this be?" He went to the girls. "Did you bring this money?"

The girls said, "No, we didn't."

He went to his wife. The Moon Lady said, "Don't ask me! Ask your daughter!"

He went to his daughter. The Sky Maiden said, "Let's see if he can come and fetch me." So the Sun Chief wrote a letter and left it on the bench.

Frog put the letter in his mouth and climbed into an empty jug. The next day, the girls carried him to earth. He jumped back into the well, and the girls went back to Heaven.

Frog brought the letter to Kimana, and Kimana read it. "You may marry my daughter if you come and fetch her."

Kimana said, "This I can't do."

Frog said, "Then I'll fetch her for you."

Kimana laughed. "I know you took a letter to Heaven and a purse of money but how can you fetch a bride?"

Frog said, "Whatever it is, I can do it. But only if I try."

Frog climbed back into the well, the girls came with their jugs and they carried him to Heaven.

Frog jumped out. He spit in all the jugs of water. *Ptui. Ptui. Ptui.* Then he hid in an empty jug.

The people of the house came and drank the water. They all got sick.

The Sun Chief called for the spirit doctor. The doctor told him, "You promised your daughter to a man of earth, but she hasn't gone. He's sent an evil spirit with a sickness and the evil spirit is in the shape of a frog."

The Sun Chief went to his wife. The Moon Lady said, "Don't ask me! Ask your daughter!"

He went to his daughter. The Sky Maiden said, "I'll go."

The next day, the Sky Maiden went with the girls down to the well.

The girls filled their jugs, and Frog jumped out. Then the girls left the Sky Maiden and went home.

Frog jumped out of the well. "I'll lead you to your husband."

The Sky Maiden laughed. "How can a frog lead a woman?"

Frog said, "I took a letter to Heaven, I took a purse of money and I fetched a bride. Whatever it was, I could do it. But only because I tried."

The Sky Maiden said, "Then it's you I'll marry."

She took Frog back to Heaven and married and they both lived happily ever after.

As for Kimana, he's still waiting for his bride.

*The traditional tale that follows is set in Mongolia. Having high aspirations is all very well and good but we also need to be aware of our limitations. If you believe you can fly like the frog in this tale, you're run the risk of landing with a nasty bump, a bump that proves fatal in this case:*

**The Flying Frog**

On the edge of beautiful Lake Hovsgol, in the north of Mongolia, there lived a flock of geese and one small frog. As autumn approached and the world grew cool, the geese began to discuss plans to fly south for the winter. The frog overheard the geese talking about the warmth and joys of southern climes, and felt sorry for himself. Shaking his head sadly, he said to the geese with bitterness:

"Oh! What a miserable life a little earthbound frog has! I'm destined to spend all my days wallowing in this cold mud! But you! How happy you geese must be to fly across the big sky, to see the world beneath you, and feel the warm sun on your backs in winter!"

The head goose felt sorry for the little frog. Winter in Mongolia was indeed brutally cold. Turning to his flock, he said:

"Brothers, we geese have wings and the frog doesn't, but we're all one family in the animal world. Let's help the frog and show him something of this wonderful world. Who can think of a way to carry the frog with us as we fly south?"

The geese consulted each other. Finally one goose picked up a willow twig and suggested:

"What about this? While the frog bites down firmly on the middle of this branch, two of us can clamp the ends in our beaks. This way we can carry the frog as we fly through the sky."

The head goose agreed to this clever idea and chose two of the biggest and strongest geese to transport the frog.

When the time came to leave, the delighted frog opened his mouth and bit firmly onto the willow branch. Off he flew, high in the sky with the flock of geese, saying goodbye to his muddy home. Looking down on the world from a great height, the frog thought to himself:

"How wonderful this is! Even though I don't have wings, I'm flying at the head of these migrating geese. How clever I am!"

For many hours the geese flew effortlessly southwards whilst the little frog hung on and marvelled at the changing sights below. As more time passed, with the refreshing wind in his face and the sun warming his back, the self-satisfied frog grew more and more confident and felt himself to be more and more powerful.

When the flock flew over an encampment of several yurts, the people herding sheep and goats below looked, pointed, and exclaimed:

"Look at that! Look at those geese! Two of them are carrying a frog on a branch. What clever geese they are!"

The people were very impressed by the intelligence of the geese and marvelled at the incredible sight until the big birds had faded out of sight. But the flying frog had heard the people's shouts of wonder and became rather irritated and jealous. He said to himself:

"Why are these geese being praised? I'm the one that's flying through the air!"

And the frog began to become resentful of the geese. Later in the afternoon, the geese flew over a small lake. The mud-bound frogs below looked up, and stared in amazement. Enviously, they all began croaking at the geese, saying:

"Hey! What about us? We want to fly too!"

The flying frog observed his cousins in the mud below with disdain and thought: "Ha! You poor devils! I'm the only frog that knows how to fly!" and he opened his boastful mouth to tell them as much:

"Hey, cousins, look at me! Flying's a piece of cake when you're as clever as I am!"

You can imagine what happened next. The moment he opened his big, bragging mouth, the flying frog slipped off the willow branch carried by two powerful geese and dropped to his death on the cold, damp earth.

*The contemporary tale chosen to conclude this chapter is actually about the fear of journeying - and the regrets we then have to live with as a result of our reluctance to step into the unknown:*

**Baa Baa Ra & Rambo**

Someone else led and Baa Baa Ra followed. That was the way it had always been and that was probably the way it would always be. That was the way the world was intended to be, or so Baa Baa Ra thought. The leader was Rambo - her husband, or the farmer, or his son-in-law, or old faithful Rover before the Annual Trials. Baa Baa Ra was one for a quiet life and always went where she was told to go. What she wanted above all was a quiet life - anything for peace and quiet was her favourite maxim and what she taught her lambs each spring. However, one day everything was about to change, as things tend to do in stories like this.

Instead of rearing the sheep for their wool, the farmer decided there was more money to be had from selling the lambs for food, and each day the size of the flock seemed to grow smaller. Rambo suggested that the only solution would be for them to all up and move in an attempt to escape from this unwelcome fate but Baa Baa Ra, as usual, saw the other side of the argument.

"I'm certain you must be mistaken. Surely he wouldn't change his ways after all these years of looking after us. The missing lambs probably just got lost."

"Rubbish!" Rambo responded, getting all hot under the collar. "Facts are facts but unfortunately you're just no prepared to face them. I know what I'm talking about. I'm older than you and I've seen it all happen before."

"But what about the poor farmer?" Baa Baa Ra interjected. "He's always treated us fairly in the past so why mistrust him now? Don't be so hasty and give him the benefit of the doubt or else you might live to regret it."

Rambo was a lone voice on this occasion and the others got their way. Reluctantly he agreed to sit back for the time being and just wait even though this was hardly his style.

However, the next week there was no escaping the fact that they were half the number they had previously been, and an Extraordinary General Meeting was called, to be held behind the old cow sheds at the far end of the field.

"You wouldn't believe me but now you can all see for yourselves that what I told you was true. We're half the number we were before and there can be no denying the fact that the farmer is selling us off to be slaughtered."

"You know you've never been good at Mathematics," Baa Baa Ra interrupted. You've probably just miscounted the flock."

There was general agreement with this suggestion, and the sheep then proceeded to make counts of their own to ascertain the facts. However, with all the baa-ing and bleating going on, it was difficult to concentrate. Everyone came up with a different number, no agreement could be reached and the meeting broke up in total confusion, with nothing being having been sorted.

Another week went by and this time there could be no denying the facts. There was clearly no mistaking the evidence because only two of them remained - Baa Baa Ra and Rambo all on their own.

"I kept telling you but you just wouldn't listen to me. If only you'd have been prepared to confront the issue, we might still be with our loved ones."

Rambo looked at his wife, expecting her to side against him as usual, but for once in her life Baa Baa Ra had no answer.

**The Ghost Woman**

In a Seneca village there was a young man who was an orphan. He had neither home nor relatives. He lived first with one family and then with another.

One fall, when the men were getting ready to go deer hunting, the young man asked if he could go. The hunters didn't want him and he was left alone. Then he said,

"I'll go by myself," and he started. Towards night he came to an opening in the woods and saw a brush house over by the bushes.

He went to the house and looked in; there was no one there. The young man thought that the other hunters had built the house and spent a night there. He went in, kindled a fire, made a place to sleep on, and lay down.

About midnight he heard someone come in and, opening his eyes, he saw a woman. She looked at him but didn't speak, then she moved toward his couch and stopped again. At last she said,

"I have come to help you. You must not be afraid. I will stay all night in the, cabin."

He said, "If you will help me, you may stay."

"I have passed through this world," said the woman, "I know that you are poor; that you have no relatives and are alone; the hunters didn't want you to go with them. This is why I came to help you. To-morrow start early and travel till it is time to camp, then I will be there."

Towards daylight the woman left the cabin.

In the morning the young man started on. Towards dark, when he thought it was time to stop, he looked for a spring, found one and had just finished his camp when night came.

In the night the woman came as before. The next day the man had good luck. He killed every kind of game.

The woman stayed with him till the hunting season was over. No hunter in the woods had killed as much game as he had. When he was ready to go home the woman said, "I will go with you to the first camp you made."

They spent the night at that camping place. The next morning, she said, "I will stay here. When you get home everybody will find out that you have brought all kinds of meat and skins. One and another will come to you and say, 'You must marry my daughter,' an old woman will say, 'You must marry my granddaughter.' Don't listen to them. Come back next year and you will have good luck. When you are getting ready, if a man wants to come with you, don't let him. Come alone. We will meet here."

They parted, and the young man continued his journey, carrying on his back a heavy load of game.

In the village he found some of the hunters. Others came soon after. All boasted of the game they had killed. The young man said,

"I will give each man as much meat as he wants, if he will go to my camp and get it."

Many went and brought back all the meat they could carry; still there was meat left.

Every woman who had a daughter or a granddaughter, asked the young man to come and live with them. At last the chief asked him to marry his daughter. The man was afraid that if he refused harm would come to him, for the chief was a powerful person. He consented and married the chief's daughter.

When the hunting season came, a great many men, and the chief, who thought his son-in-law was the best hunter in the tribe, wanted to go hunting with him, but he said, "I'm not going, this year."

The hunters started off one after another. When all had gone, the young man went alone to the camp where he was to meet the woman.

Early in the night she came in, stopped by the door, and said, "I am sorry you didn't do as I told you to. I cannot stay with you," and she disappeared.

Day after day the man hunted but he saw no large game. He shot small game, squirrels and birds, for he was hungry. He went back to the village and had to tell the people that he had seen no game.

The woman was a ghost woman.[9]

*Recognize and listen to your Helpers from other realities or, like the young man in this story, ghosts will be all that you are left with, ghosts to remind you of what might have been, and your dreams will come to nothing too.*

---

9 The story chosen to close this collection is taken from *Seneca Indian Myths* collected by Jeremiah Curtin, New York: E.P. Dutton & Company (1922). Scanned at sacred-texts.com, July 2004. Redacted by John Bruno Hare. This text is in the public domain in the United States. These files may be used for any non-commercial purposes, provided this notice of attribution is left intact.

## Chapter 14
## SOUL LOSS, SOUL POSSESSION AND SOUL CAPTIVATION

The soul, in certain spiritual, philosophical and psychological traditions, is the incorporeal essence of a person or living thing. Many philosophical and spiritual systems teach that humans are souls; some attribute souls to all living things and even to inanimate objects (such as rivers); this belief is commonly called animism, and in shamanism all life is considered to be connected in this respect too. The soul is often believed to exit the body and live on after a person's death, and some religions posit that God creates souls. The soul has often been deemed integral or essential to consciousness and personality, and is used as a synonym for spirit.

In shamanism soul loss is the term used to describe the way parts of that essence become detached when we are faced with traumatic situations. In psychological terms, it is known as dissociation and it works as a defence mechanism, a means of displacing unpleasant feelings, impulses or thoughts into the unconscious. In shamanic terms, these split off parts can be found in non-ordinary reality and are only accessible to those familiar with its topography (see Gagan, 1998, p.9). Soul retrieval entails the shaman journeying to find the missing parts and then returning them to the client seeking help. The shaman, in the words of Eliade, "is the great specialist in the human soul: he alone 'sees' it, for he knows its 'form' and its destiny" (Eliade, 1989, p.8). What we are concerned with though, can perhaps best be described as a case of soul captivation or even soul theft rather than case of soul loss.

Soul Captivation is not to be confused with Charismatic Captivation, a term used to refer to the widespread problem of authoritarian abuse in some Neo-Pentecostal church-groups that permeated the very fabric, foundation, and functions of the Neo-Pentecostal church after being introduced through a Charismatic campaign known as the Discipleship/Shepherding Movement (1970-77) [see http://www.charismatic-captivation.com]. Neither is Soul Captivation to be confused with the more commonly referred to Soul Possession, which is what we shall start by considering.

Soul Possession is a paranormal/supernatural event in which, allegedly, spirits, gods, demons, or other disincarnate or extraterrestrial entities take control of a human body, resulting in noticeable changes in the health and behaviour of the affected person. The term can also describe a similar action of taking residence in an inanimate object, such as in the case of the Golem of Prague, thereby giving it animation. Possession may be voluntary or involuntary and may be considered to have beneficial or detrimental effects.

In Haitian Vodou, for example, practitioners can be possessed by the *lwa* (or Loa). When the *lwa* descends upon a practitioner, the practitioner's body is being used by the spirit, according to the tradition. Some spirits are believed to be able to give prophecies of upcoming events or situations pertaining to the possessed one, also called *Chwal* or the 'Horse of the Spirit'. After the event, the practitioner has no recollection of the possession and not all practitioners have the ability to become possessed, but practitioners who do generally prefer not to make excessive use of it because it leaves them feeling drained.

In Christian orthodoxy, cast-down angels, or demons are disembodied angels and are able to 'demonically possess' individuals. Christians believe that there are many spirits in the world, but only the Holy Spirit is considered pure and trustworthy. They see the human body as having been created to be a temple to the living God. They also believe Jesus came to the earth to fill all things with His Holy Spirit, which is the fullness of God literally living inside of a believer.

In the Jewish tradition, possession can take the form of a *dybuk.* After three reincarnations without repair, the soul is not permitted to be reincarnated any more as a human being, and may be reincarnated only in a sub-human form. However, in very extreme cases, a soul may not even be permitted transmigration.

Prohibited from the spiritual realm, it is thrust back into the physical world with no 'body'. There, demons and spirits pursue the bodiless soul as it frantically seeks refuge from their torment. Sometimes it finds respite in a sub-human host, such as an animal, plant or inanimate object. This is different than transmigration, though, since it is not placed there with the potential for repair, rather it invades the object from without, merely seeking refuge in 'exile'.

Another possibility is that it finds 'room' in another person's body. Usually this happens when the desperate soul finds a spiritual 'breach' in a person. ... Once a soul enters such a 'breach', it cleaves tenaciously to its human host who shelters it from its pursuers. This 'cleaving', or possession, called a *dybuk,* usually takes over the person's speech and behaviour.

...A second reason for *dybuk* is premature death. ... This can result in a prematurely disconnected soul that has not yet lived out its purpose in this world. As a result, it refrains from undergoing reincarnation, which would initiate a new life. Rather, it clings to this world seeking to fulfil its unrealized potential in its current life by cleaving to another person's body.

Whether the *dybuk* occurs because of punishment or premature death, it can be removed by exorcism, which is a spiritual reparation whereby a tainted soul publicly confesses the sins of its previous life, or a prematurely parted soul is promised fulfilment; each case is accompanied by the spiritual influences of a Kabbalistic ceremony (taken from www.RabbiuUllman.com ).

At certain times, the risk of becoming possessed was considered to be greater than at others, such as at night time.

...Enhancing the fear of demons at night was the realization that man's vigilance is relaxed while he sleeps; even more, the soul having left the body, that both body and soul are peculiarly open to attack.

... Great as the danger was every night of the week, on two nights especially was it heightened—the eves of Wednesday and Saturday. At these times hordes of peculiarly devastating spirits were let loose upon the world. During the Talmudic period Friday night in particular was considered an unhealthy time to be abroad alone, and the rabbis required that no man be left behind in the synagogue to finish his prayers alone after the congregation had concluded the service and gone home. For then he must negotiate the distance to his home without a companion (Trachtenberg, 1939, pp.46-47).

At certain critical stages of life one had to be on one's guard too.

These were the moments in the life cycle "when man's star is low": birth, illness, death, while marriage, man's happiest moment, was an especially perilous one. These were the moments of man's greatest vulnerability when the struggle with the spirits grew intense. And just these were the occasions selected by the sorcerer as most propitious for his sinister work, the junctures when the curse and the evil eye took their greatest toll (ibid. pp.47-48).

As for the widespread belief in the Middle Ages that at the moment of death a struggle ensues between the angels and the devil over the soul of the deceased, it was paralleled in Jewish thought by the notion that the demons seek to gain possession of the corpse while it is yet unburied.

The corpse itself was also an object of fear. The dead had entered the world of the spirits, the soul hovered over its vacated shell, potentially capable of harming those who came near. For this reason contact with the dead was to be avoided, and the clothing of the deceased was not to be used again, "because of the danger." Indeed, fear of the soul and the spirits, and apprehension that the demons might do harm to the deceased, was the explanation advanced for the prohibition to leave a corpse unburied overnight. The sooner the body was out of the way the better for the living and the dead (ibid. pp.48-49).

As for Wiccans, they believe in voluntary possession by the Goddess, connected with the sacred ceremony of Drawing down the Moon. The high priestess solicits the Goddess to possess her and speak thrugh her.

Soul Captivation, on the other hand, involves the enchantment of the affected person to such an extent that they become slaves to their emotions, and then act in what society would regard as an unbalanced manner in their relationships with those they come into contact with.

A shamanic journey is one that generally takes place in a trance state to the sound of a drumbeat, through dancing, or by ingesting psychoactive drugs, in which aid is sought from beings in (what are considered to be) other realities generally for healing purposes or for divination - both for individuals and/or the community. A shamanic story can be defined as one that has either been based on or inspired by a shamanic journey, or one that contains a number of the elements typical of such a journey. The shamanic story about soul captivation that follows comes from the Republic of Georgia.

**The Earth will take its Own**

There lived a certain widow and she had an only son. The son grew up and saw that only he had nobody he could call father.

"Why does everybody else have a father and only I don't have one?" he asked his mother.

"Your father died".

"What does it mean *died*? Does it mean that he won't come back to us anymore?"

"He won't come back to us but we'll all go there - to where he is", said his mother. "Nobody can run away from death".

The young man said, "I didn't ask anybody for life, but I'm already alive and I don't want to die. I'm going to find such a place where they don't die".

For a long time his mother begged him not to go, but her son did not listen, and he set out to look for such a place where they do not die. He went round the whole world. And wherever he went, he asked the same question, "Is there death here?"

"There is", they answered him.

The young man became sad: there is no such place where they do not die. On one occasion, when he was walking across a plain, he saw a deer with high branching antlers. The young man liked the deer's antlers very much, and he asked the deer, "Don't you know somewhere where they don't die?"

"There's no such place", said the deer, "but until my antlers grow up to the sky, I won't die; but when they grow up that high, my death will come too. If you like, stay with me and you won't die while I'm alive".

"No", said the young man, "either I want to live eternally, or I might just as well die where I come from".

The young man went on further. He crossed the plain, he went all through the valleys and reached the mountains. He saw a raven sitting on a crag, cleaning himself, and shedding his downy feathers into a huge deep gorge below. The young man asked the raven, "Don't you know a place where they don't die?"

"No", said the raven. "Here I'll live until all of this gorge is filled with my downy feathers, but when it's filled, then I'll die. Stay with me and live on until the time when I die".

The young man looked into the gorge and shook his head. "No", he said, "either I want to live eternally or I might just as well die where I come from".

The young man went on further. He passed through the whole world, and approached the sea. He walked along the shore, not knowing where to go. One day passed, two days passed, but nothing could be seen. On the third day he saw something shining in the distance. He walked towards it and there stood a crystal castle. The young man walked around the castle, but he could not find any kind of door. For a long time he was tormented, but at last he noticed a small streak, and he guessed that this was really the entrance. He pressed with all his strength and the door opened. The young man went inside and saw, lying there, a young woman of such beauty that the sun itself would envy her if it saw her.

The young man liked the woman a lot and she fancied him too. The young man asked, "Beautiful lady, I want to get away from death. Don't you know a place where they don't die?"

"There's no such place", said the young woman, "why waste your time looking for it? Stay here with me instead".

He said, "I wasn't looking for you, I'm looking for such a place where they don't die, otherwise I would have stayed there, where I have come from".

The young woman said, "The earth will take its own, you yourself would not want to be immortal. Come, tell me, how old am I?"

The young man looked at her: Her fresh cheeks, the colour of roses, were so beautiful that he completely forgot about death. "Fifteen years old at the very most", he said.

"No", answered the young woman, "I was created on the first day of the beginning of the world. They call me Krasoy, and I will never become old and will never die. You would be able to stay with me forever, but you will not want to-the earth will call you". The young man swore that he would never leave her.

They began to live together. The years flew past, like a moment. Much changed on the earth. Many died. They turned into dust. Many were born. The earth changed its face, but the young man did not notice how the time had flown. The young woman was always just as beautiful, and he was always just as young. Thousands of years flew past.

The young man missed his old home, and he wanted to visit his people. He said, "I want to go and see my mother and family".

She said, "Even their bones no longer remain in the earth".

He said, "What are you talking about! Altogether I've only been here for three or four days. What could have happened to them?"

The young woman said, "As I've been telling you, the earth will take its own. All right, go then! But remember that whatever happens to you, you've only got yourself to blame". She gave him three apples and told him to eat them when he started to feel miserable.

The young man said goodbye to her and went. He walked, and he walked, and he saw the crag that the raven had been sitting on. The young man looked: all the gorge was filled up with his downy feathers, and there was the raven himself, lying all dried up. It grew dark in the young man's eyes, and he wanted to go back again, but already the earth would not allow him, it drew him forward. He went further, and he saw, standing on the plain, the deer. His antlers reached the sky, and the deer himself was dying. The young man realised that much time has passed since he left home. He went on further. He reached the area where he had been born, but he did not find either relatives or acquaintances. He asked people about his mother, but nobody had even heard of her. He walked alone and nobody knew him.

At last he met a certain old man, and told him who he was looking for. The old man said, "That woman, as I heard from my grandfather and great-grandfather, lived once; but how could her son be alive now?" There went through the whole land the rumour about this person. But what they say about him! They regard him as some kind of freak.

The young man carried on walking alone. He came to that place where once there stood his home, and he found only ruins, which were already reddened with moss. The young man remembered his mother, his childhood, his companions, and he became sad. He decided to eat the apples that the young woman from the crystal castle had given him. He got out one apple, ate it, and suddenly there grew on his face a long grey beard. He ate the second apple, and his knees gave way, the small of his back bent and he fell to the ground without any strength. He was lying there, unable to move either an arm or a leg. He called a passing boy, "Come close to me, Boy. Get the apple out of my pocket and give it to me". The boy got the apple, and gave it to him. He took a bite of it and he died right then and there.

The entire village community came to bury him.

*What we learn from the above tale, and also the one that follows, is that not all shamanic journeys have successful conclusions, and not all those who undertake such journeys are necessarily able to find their way home again after their quests. For some unfortunate beings, there is no release from soul captivation; they remain the prisoners of their temptations forever.*

**The Enchanted Lake**

In the west of Ireland there was a lake, and no doubt it is there still, in which many young men had been at various times drowned. What made the circumstance remarkable was that the bodies of tile drowned persons were never found. People naturally wondered at this: and at length the lake came to have a bad repute. Many dreadful stories were told about that lake; some would affirm, that on a dark night its waters appeared like fire - others would speak of horrid forms which were seen to glide over it; and everyone agreed that a strange sulphurous smell issued from out of it.

There lived, not far distant from this lake, a young farmer, named Roderick Keating, who was about to be married to one of the prettiest girls in that part of the country. On his return from Limerick, where he had been to purchase the wedding-ring, he came up with two or three of his acquaintance, who were standing on the shore, and they began to joke with him about

Peggy Honan. One said that young Delaney, his rival, had in his absence contrived to win the affection of his mistress ; - but Roderick's confidence in his intended bride was too great to be disturbed at this tale, and putting his hand in his pocket, he produced and held up with a significant look the wedding-ring. As he was turning it between his fore-finger and thumb, in token of triumph, somehow or other the ring fell from his hand, and rolled into the lake: Roderick looked after it with the greatest sorrow; it was not so much for its value, though it had cost him half-a-guinea, as for the ill-luck of the thing; and the water was so deep, that there was little chance of recovering it. His companions laughed at him, and he in vain endeavoured to tempt any of them by the offer of a handsome reward to dive after the ring: they were all as little inclined to venture as Roderick Keating himself; for the tales which they had heard when children were strongly impressed on their memories, and a superstitious dread filled the mind of each.

"Must I then go back to Limerick to buy another ring?" exclaimed the young farmer.

"Will not ten times what the ring cost tempt any one of you to venture after it?"

There was within hearing a man who was considered to be a poor, crazy, half-witted fellow, but he was as harmless as a child, and used to go wandering up and down through the country from one place to another. When he heard of so great a reward; Paddeen, for that was his name, spoke out, and said, that if Roderick Keating would give him encouragement equal to what he had offered to others, he was ready to venture after the ring into the lake; and Paddeen, all the while he spoke, looked as covetous after the sport as .the money.

"I'll take you at your word," said Keating. So Paddeen pulled off his coat, and without a single syllable more, down he plunged, head fore-most, into the lake: what depth he went to, no one can tell exactly; but he was going, going, going down through the water, until the water parted from him, and he came upon the dry land; the sky, and the light, and everything, was there just as it is here; and he saw fine pleasure-grounds, with an elegant avenue through them, and a grand house, with a power of steps going up to the door. When he had recovered from his wonder at finding the land so dry and comfortable under the water, he looked about him and what should he see but all the young men that were drowned working away in the pleasure-grounds as if nothing bad ever happened to them. Some of them were mowing down the grass, and more were settling out the gravel walks, and doing all manner of nice work, as neat and as clever as if they had never been drowned; and they were singing away with high glee:

*"She is fair as Cappoquin :*
*Have you courage her to win ?*
*And her wealth it far outshines*
*Cullen's bog and Silvermines.*
*She exceeds all heart can wish;*
*Not brawling like the Foherish,*
*But as the brightly-flowing Lee,*
*Graceful, mild, and pure is she! "*

Well, Paddeen could not but look at the young men, for he knew some of them before they were lost in the lake; but he said nothing, though he thought a great deal more for all that, like an oyster : - no, not the wind of a word passed his lips; so on he went towards the big house, bold enough, as if he had seen nothing to speak of; yet all the time mightily wishing to know who the young woman could be that the young men were singing the song about.

When he had nearly reached the door of the great house, out walks from the kitchen a powerful fat woman, moving along like a beer-barrel on two legs, with teeth as big as horses' teeth, and up she made towards him.

"Good morrow, Paddeen," said she.

"Good morrow, Ma'am," said he.

"What brought you here?" said she.

" 'Tis after Rory Keating's gold ring," said he, " I'm come."

"Here it is for you," said Paddeen's fat friend, with a smile on her face that moved like boiling stirabout [gruel].

"Thank you, Ma'am," replied Paddeen, taking it from her: -" I need not say the Lord increase you, for you are fat enough already. Will you tell me, if you please, am I to go back the same way I came?"

"Then you did not come to marry me?" cried the corpulent woman, in a desperate fury.

"Just wait till I come back again, my darling," said Paddeen: "I'm to be paid for my message, and I must return with the answer, or else they'll wonder what has become of me."

"Never mind the money," said the fat woman: "if you marry me, you shall live for ever and a day in that house, and want for nothing."

Paddeen saw clearly that, having got possession of the ring, the fat woman had no power to detain him; so without minding anything she said, he kept moving and moving down the avenue, quite quietly, and looking about him; for, to tell the truth, he had no particular inclination to marry a fat fairy. When he came to the gate, without ever saying goodbye, out he bolted, and he found the water coming all about him again. Up he plunged through it, and wonder enough there was, when Paddeen was seen swimming away at the opposite side of the lake; but he soon made the shore, and told Roderick Keating, and the other boys that were standing there looking out for him, all that had happened. Roderick paid him the five guineas for the ring on the spot; and Paddeen thought himself so rich with such a sum of money in his pocket, that he did not go back to marry the fat lady with the fine house at the bottom of the lake, knowing she had plenty of young men to choose a husband from, if she pleased to be married.

Taken from *Fairy Legends and Traditions* by Thomas Crofton Croker [1825] at www.sacred-texts.com

**References**

Berman, M. *The Nature of Shamanism and the Shamanic Story*, Newcastle: Cambridge Scholars Publishing [for *The Earth will take its Own*].

Eliade, M. (1989) *Shamanism: Archaic techniques of ecstasy*, London: Arkana (first published in the USA by Pantheon Books 1964).

Gagan, J.M. (1998) *Journeying: where shamanism and psychology meet*, Santa Fe, NM: Rio Chama Pubications.

Trachtenberg, T. (1939) *Jewish Magic and Superstition: A Study in Folk Religion*, New York: Behrman's Jewish Book House. Scanned, proofed and formatted by John Bruno Hare at sacred-texts.com, January 2008. This text is in the public domain in the US because its copyright was not renewed in a timely fashion at the US Copyright office as required by law at the time.

## Appendix 1
## DISCUSSION POINTS FOR STORYTELLING GROUPS AND THE CLASSROOM

**The Pouch Full of Gold** (page 53)
Read through the story and then choose the most suitable moral for it. (If none of the suggested morals seem appropriate to you, then write a moral of your own).

- Crime doesn't pay.
- One good turn deserves another.
- It takes a thief to catch a thief
- An eye for an eye and a tooth for a tooth
- Honesty is the best policy.
- All's Fair in Love and War.

**Growing Old** (page 54)
They say that young people today have no respect for the older generation. Do you agree or is it perhaps different in your country? And can we learn from the experience of others or is it true that we can only learn from our own mistakes? What do you think?

**Solomon the Wise and the Hermit** (page 55)
The story can be used to practise predictive skills. Stop reading after the sentence “The sweepings stand for our earthly possessions”, and then ask the listeners, working in groups, to work out, in the same way, the meaning of the other three signs - the hermit standing at the threshold, the cloth over his shoulders, and the hermit holding his mouth. Then, after you show or read the rest of the tale to them, they can compare their interpretations with the original.

**The King Who Would See Paradise** (page 56)

Working in small groups, try to agree on the most appropriate moral for the tale, and give reasons for the choice you make. (If you feel none of the morals are appropriate, feel free to choose one of your own). Then you might like to explain why you consider the other options to be unsuitable:

- Ignorance is bliss
- All that glitters is not gold
- Curiosity killed the cat
- Forbidden fruit is sweetest
- All good things come to those who wait
- A word is enough to the wise
- Fools rush in where wise men fear to tread

**The Treasure at Home** (page 76)

*Post-listening:* Pause after the words "Isaac turned around and went home, where he took his oven apart and found …" and ask the listeners to predict the ending.

Have you ever searched far and wide for a solution to a problem that was actually under your very nose all the time? Tell me about it.

If you found a chest of treasure, what would you do with it and why?

**The Daydreamer** (page 77)

How much time do you spend daydreaming and what do you daydream about?

How would you describe yourself - are you the sort of person who spends all their time talking about what they plan to do or are you the sort of person who believes in acting? In your opinion, which sort of person is more likely to be successful?

**The Confirmation** (page 81)

*Pre-listening:* Listen to the story to find out where the experience took place.

*Post-listening:* If someone who was once important to you came back into your life again, what message do you think they would like to pass on to you, and why? (Or) What do you think you need to remember, based on the experiences you've had, that you unfortunately keep forgetting? Tell the person sitting next to you all about it.

**The Story of the Hyacinth** (page 94)
*Post-listening:* (You might like to play some soothing background music while reading the following script to create a suitable atmosphere) Make yourselves comfortable and take a few deep breaths to help you relax. Breathe in the white light and breathe out all your tightness. Take a minute of clock time, equal to all the time you need, to take a look at your Book of Life, to see what the future has in store for you ... Now turn to the person sitting next to you. Take it in turns to talk about what you saw in the Book, what you liked or disliked about it, and what changes you plan to make to ensure the future turns out the way you want it to be.

**The Bamboo Princess** (page 95)
*Post-listening:* What's the most precious thing you've ever lost in your life? Was there anything you could have done to prevent this from happening? How did you learn to live with your pain? Why do you think it is that we so often lose what we value the most? Tell the person sitting next to you about your experiences or talk about them together in groups.

**Winter Bamboo Shoots** (page 97)
*Pre-listening:* If you were about to die and you could have one final meal beforehand, what would it be and why? Now listen to find out what the woman in the story chose.
*Post-listening:* Is it our duty to look after our parents when they grow old or should we put them into an Old People's Home?

**The Origin of Xian-Fei Bamboo** (page 98)
Xianfei bamboo is covered with black spots that look like tears. The Yellow River flows through the provinces of Henan and Shandong to the north of Hunan Province. Da Yu is a semi-mythical figure said to have begun his heroic exploits in 2297 B.C. and the first of the Yellow River's dike builders. Dongting Lake, where the story takes place, is the setting for many Chinese folktales. I wonder whether you would have put your country before your partner in the same way that Da Yu did. This could provide an interesting point for discussion as a post-listening activity.

As a post-listening activity, the following questions could be discussed in pairs or small groups: Looking back through the history of your country, which monarch or leader do you feel genuinely cared for and looked after the people? Give reasons for the choices you make. If you had been one of Yu-

Sun's wives, how long would you have been prepared to wait for him? Was the loyalty of Erh-Huang and Nu-Ying something to admire or was it misplaced? What do you think? How do you feel about men being able to have more than one wife, or women being able to have more than one husband? Do you think it is possible to love more than one person at the same time?

**The Lily of the Valley** (page 100)
This traditional tale comes from Romania. As a post-listening activity, the following questions could be discussed in pairs or small groups: "Heartbroken and driven half crazy with grief, Margarita strangled the Khan with her belt and pushed him over the cliff." Can murder ever be justified - what do you think? When there are extenuating circumstances as in the case of Margarita, should these be taken into account by the judge when sentencing or are they irrelevant? *Tartar's Cliff* and *the Rock of Death* - Are there any interesting stories that explain the origin of place names in your country?

**The Legend of the Lily** (page 101)
The legend, which comes from Romania, could lead into parallel story writing - with the participants working individually or collaboratively in groups: What other stories do you know about witches, forests and dragons? How about trying to write one of your own, incorporating all three elements? Will the hero / heroine die at the end of the tale or will there be a happy ending?

**The Singing Rose** (page 102)
As a post-listening activity, the following questions could be discussed in pairs or small groups: If you had been the old king, how would you have chosen which of your daughters to make queen? How would you have felt if you had been one of the daughters not chosen by your father, the king? What's the most heavenly sound that you have ever heard? If you had been the old man, what would you have done with your singing roses? Why do you think grumbling greybeard did not want his beautiful wife to smile or speak at her sisters' weddings?

The following title could be used to facilitate a piece of creative writing: Imagine you are the youngest daughter of the king and married to grumbling greybeard. Write a letter to your husband explaining how you feel and asking him to free you from your vows.

**Echo and Narcissus** (page 106)
As a post-listening activity, the following questions could be discussed in pairs or small groups: When you have an argument with your partner, who usually has the last word - you, your partner, or you hardly ever quarrel with each other? How much time do you spend looking at yourself in the mirror every day? Do you think it is true that women generally spend more time doing this than men? How important is your appearance to you and what do you do to preserve your looks? Would you ever be prepared to consider having cosmetic surgery, for example? How do you fell about people who resort to this?

You might also like to find out whether the participants are familiar with any other Greek myths and if they can tell them to you and / or each other.

**The Princess of Seven Jasmines** (page 107)
*The Princess of Seven Jasmines* is a fairy tale from India. You can invite the participants to listen to the story to find out what the moral is. If the prince had not shown compassion towards the seven-hooded snake, the ants and the giant, he would probably never have received the help he needed to succeed in the tasks the king set him.

As a post-listening activity, the following questions could be discussed in pairs or small groups: They say that one good turn deserves another - how far has this been true in your life? What examples can you think of to illustrate the truth that lies behind this maxim? Is it right to give in the hope of receiving something good in return? Some people say that charity begins at home - how far do you agree with this?

**The Princess Peony** (page 112)
As a post-listening activity, the following questions could be discussed in pairs or small groups: The marriage of Princess Aya to Lord Ako's second son was arranged by their parents. How would you feel about having your partner chosen for you? If you had been O Sadayo, would you have told tales to the Lord or would you have kept what you had been told privately a secret? The handsome young samurai was supposedly the spirit of the Peony flower. Can flowers have spirits or feelings - what do you think? Some people claim their plants grow better if they talk to them each day or play them music. Have you ever tried this?

**The Iris** (page 116)
*Post-listening:* If you could be turned into a flower, which one would you choose to be and why? How much luck do you feel you've had in your life - less than you fair share, more than your fair share, or just about an average amount? What would you rather have - luck or mind? Give reasons for the choice you make. What faculty would you least like to lose and why? Which extra talent would you most like to have, and why?

**How the Crocus got its Fur Coat** (page 118)
Wapee goes on what is known as a Vision Quest. Find out what other Native American practices participants are familiar with. What about the Sweat Lodge or the Sun Dance Ceremony? If you have access to computers, this information could be found through a search on the internet.

**The Love of the South Wind for the Dandelion** (page 120)
Shawondasee admired the slender 'girl' from a distance, waited too long without acting, and lost her. Have you ever made this mistake in life? Tell me about it.

**It's all in the _____** (page 121)
Have you ever struggled like the man in the story to leave the past behind you? How did you succeed in the end? Tell the person sitting next to you all about it.

Suggested Answer: It's all in the Mind

**How Tamerlane found his Fortune** (page 122)
*Pre-listening*: Tell the person sitting next to you about a dream you've had that changed your life in some way, or about a remarkable dream that somebody you know had.
*While-listening*: Pause after the words "Then after digging up the very same spot where the soul of the blacksmith had crawled, Temir exposed…" and ask the learners to predict the ending.
*Post-listening*: Now invite the learners, while working in groups, to write a parallel story about a fly that crawls out of someone's nose, the journey it goes on, and the discovery that journey eventually leads to for the dreamer.

**Learning the Hard Way**
Place the following sentences in the correct order to make a parable, and then

discuss, in pairs or small groups, whether learning the hard way is the only way to learn, from our own mistakes, or whether perhaps there is another less painful way:

a. "Father," he cried angrily, "Why did you lock me in that closet?

b. Hours later, his son returned home, bedraggled and exhausted.

c. If I hadn't been made desperate by my fear of getting caught, I never would have escaped. It took all my ingenuity to get out!"

d. The father told his son to go into the closet to pick out some clothes.

e. Then he went back outside, knocked loudly on the front door, thereby waking the family, and quickly slipped away before anyone saw him.

f. The old thief smiled. "Son, you've just had your first lesson in the art of burglary."

g. The son of a master thief asked his father to teach him the secrets of the trade.

h. The old thief agreed and that night took his son to burgle a large house.

i. When he did, his father quickly shut the door and locked him in.

j. While the family was asleep, he silently led his young apprentice into a room that contained a clothes closet.

ANSWERS: 1-g / 2-h / 3-j / 4-d / 5-i / 6- e / 7-b / 8-a / 9-c / 10-f

**The After-Life, and the Banquet of the King** (page 124)
*Pre-listening*: Imagine you were invited to a banquet at Buckingham Palace and the invitation said you had to bring your own seat with you to sit on. How would you feel about this, and what would you take with for the purpose?
*Post-listening*: Perhaps you will say that you have this at my hands. It is not so; but you yourselves have made all this for yourselves, therefore, "you shall lie down in sorrow" ((Is. l. 11), "it is at your own hands that you suffer all

this." The condition of your souls in the life to come, in the banquet of eternal splendour that God has provided, will be such as you prepare for yourselves (Taken from *Midrash Koheleth*).

But are we in fact entirely responsible for what we have in this world? Do people become poor of their own making or is society perhaps responsible for the predicament they find themselves in? What do you think?

**The Peacemaker** (page 124)

*Pre-listening:* If war broke out tomorrow and it involved your country in some way, would you enlist or be a conscientious objector? Give reasons for the choice you make.

*Post-listening:* The following questions could be discussed in pairs or small groups:

a. Is it ever worth risking your life for something you believe in passionately? Are such people brave heroes or simply rash idiots? What do you think?

b. How do you feel about compulsory military service? Does it provide young people with a useful education and a chance to see the world or is it nothing more than a complete waste of time? And should it be for both sexes or only for men?

c. If you think that military service should be done away with, what would you like to see in its place?

d. How do you behave in disagreements with colleagues, your immediate family, or your partner? Who usually says sorry first - you, the other party, or is it perhaps the case that you hardly ever find yourself in such situations?

e. What sort of relationships do you now have with people you have fallen out with in the past?

f. What do you find to be an effective way of dealing with any conflicts you have to face? Are there any special techniques that you can perhaps recommend?

**The Importance of__** (page 125)

Have you ever been sent a sign that you failed to notice, or have you ever been offered a helping hand that you failed to take advantage of? Tell the person sitting next to you about it.

Suggested Answer: The Importance of Faith

**The Scorpion and the Frog** (page 129)

*Pre-listening:* Can people change their natures? What do you think? The story of *The Scorpion and the Frog* offers a possible answer to this question.

*Post-listening:* Pause after the words "The scorpion shrugged did a little jig on the drowning frog's back, and replied …" and ask the listeners to predict the ending.

## Appendix 2
## THE STORY AS A CEREMONY

Cahill and Halpern (1991) suggest that there are three distinct stages in ceremony which need to be honoured for the experience to touch us deeply: Severance - leaving behind the everyday world, entering Sacred Time & Space - going beyond ourselves, and Reincorporation - returning with new self-knowledge. As these are the same psychological processes that compose our lives, there is a strong case to be made for following the same steps when telling a story in class.

Einstein famously remarked that we cannot solve problems from within the mind frame that created the problems in the first place. Any time that we step outside our assumptions or habitual way of seeing things by entering Sacred Time & Space, we are experiencing what Zohar (2000) calls our SQ (Spiritual Intelligence) and to some small extent, at least, using it for the purpose of self-development.

Entering the ritual space can be compared to entering a temple because it serves as a focusing lens. When we enter marked-off space everything, at least potentially, assumes significance and even the ordinary becomes sacred by having our attention directed to it in a special way (see Smith, 1982, pp.54-55).

Reincorporation, like recollection, entails the bringing together of our world inside and our world outside, the meeting of the deep, inner self and its innate wisdom or spiritual intelligence with the outer ego and its worldly concerns, strategies and activities. Recollection can be defined as SQ in action. And what Emile Durkheim wrote about ritual in connection with religion, can apply just as well to the lesson:

Once we are acquitted of our ritual duties, [in other words, once the ceremony is complete] we re-enter profane life with more courage and enthusiasm, not only because we have put ourselves in touch with a higher source of energy, but also because our forces have been reinvigorated by living briefly a life that is more relaxed, more free and easy. In this way, religion has a charm that is not the least of its attractions Durkheim, 2001, p.285).

However, it should be pointed out that this can only be achieved by creating the right kind of conditions, in which the learners can feel relaxed and thus able to produce their best work.

Mention should also be made of the power of ritual to bring people together, to create what Victor Turner refers to as "communitas", something that is recognised by Rappaport (1979) too. He notes that one of the benefits to be derived from rituals is that they can alter consciousness by inducing a feeling of "loss of self", that sense of separation we often experience in our daily lives, and they thus enable us to experience a feeling of union with other members of the congregation [class]. Driver refers to the power of ritual to bring people together too:

Three stages of ritual can be identified - preliminal, liminal and post-liminal. And the liminality of ritual can be regarded as 'a recourse from society's alienating structures to a generalized bond of unity … that is felt or intuited among humans and other beings' (Driver, 1991, p.162).

In a story telling session, you leave the everyday world behind you the moment the storyteller says *once upon a time,* you're transported beyond yourself into another setting during the telling of the tale, and you return with new self-knowledge if the story worked as a metaphor for you.

Through guided imagery, you can leave behind the stress of daily life through relaxation, you go beyond yourself by entering a light state of trance, and you return with the visions you had on your journey.

In a role play, you can leave behind the everyday world by taking on a new identity. You can go beyond yourself when you act out the part, and you return with new self-knowledge by discovering the kind of performance you're capable of and perhaps by gaining a deeper insight into the nature of the character you portray.

So the next time you plan or analyze a lesson, see whether the three stages described in this model can be applied to it. If they can't, then perhaps there is something missing - a vital ingredient that could make it work better.

***References***

Cahill, S., & Halpern, J. (1991) *The Ceremonial Circle Shamanic Practice, Ritual and Renewal*, London: Mandala.

Driver, T.F. (1991) *The Magic of Ritual*, New York: Harper Collins Publishers.

Durkheim, E. (2001) *The Elementary Forms of Religious Life*, Oxford: Oxford University Press (originally published in 1912).
Smith, J.Z. (1982) *Imagining Religion: From Babylon to Jonestown*, Chicago: University of Chicago Press.
Turner, V. (1995) *The Ritual Process: Structure and Anti-Structure*, Chicago, Illinois: Aldine Publishing Company (first published in 1969).
Van Gennep, A. (1977) *The Rites of Passage*, London: Routledge and Keegan Paul (original work published in 1909).
Zohar, H., & Marshall, I. (2000) *Spiritual Intelligence The Ultimate Intelligence*, London: Bloomsbury.

